# CHOOSING UP

MOSAICA PRESS

Ilana Kendal

CHOOSING UP

Elevating
the Everyday

Published by Mosaica Press, Inc.
www.mosaicapress.com
info@mosaicapress.com

To Mom and Dad,
for always believing in me.

## THE CENTER FOR KEHILLAH DEVELOPMENT
*Ramat HaGolan St. 21b, Ramat Eshkol, Yerushalayim*

August 2, 2018

Ilana Kendal is more than just an exceedingly humble person with especially refined character. She is wise, wise far beyond her years. She earned that wisdom through personal struggle and perseverance, and today she is a voice worth paying attention to. We are fortunate that she has allowed us into her internal world. Most people will find the visit there all too brief, and will hope she continues to share more in years to come.

*Leib Kelemen*
Rosh HaKollel

# Rabbi Paysach J. Krohn

117-09 85th Avenue • Kew Gardens, NY 11418          (718) 846-6900 • Fax (718) 846-6903
e-mail: krohnmohel@brisquest.com • www.brisquest.com

Tu B'shvat 5779
January 2019

Dear Reader,

As you begin to turn the pages of this book, know that you are about to begin a journey – an expedition into Hashem's world of the obvious and His meticulous world of subtleties. In this profound work of perceptions and insights, you will be delighted not only by what the author makes you see, but also by the choice of words, expressions and sentence structure on just about every page.

In my youth, my late mother, Mrs. Hindy Krohn, who taught me the appreciation of word usage, encouraged me to underline wondrous turns of phrases and clever combinations of words in the newspapers and magazines we read together. If I had this book in those years, I would be underlining numerous times on every page.

Here are some examples, "Experiencing self-control is the birthplace of personal power." "We will be defined by who we are in the privacy of our homes." Ilana is a teacher, guide and mentor who shows us how to appreciate the seemingly unglamorous moments of life and realize there are wise lessons inherent in those moments.

The encounter in a restaurant with an elderly lady at the next table, observing a firefighter in the heat of flames, the wilting flower in someone's garden, the flagman on a public roadway steering traffic – all become entities of micro-moments with maxi-lessons. This is a book to be read and re-read, to be studied and absorbed – so that it will change and elevate your life.

I have been getting Ilana's columns for years. I look forward to them every Friday. I am so glad they now are together in book form. She has performed a great service – and you, the reader will be the grateful benefactor.

Respectfully,

Rabbi Paysach J. Krohn

# Table of Contents

# Acknowledgments

I t is an impossible task to acknowledge all who have contributed to making the dream of this book a reality. As a child, whenever I struggled, my mother would say, "Someday this will be in your book." I have carried this perspective throughout my life, and been blessed to have decades of supporters, teachers, and friends who have guided this work. Doubtless I have neglected to mention someone here, and for that I ask forgiveness.

The ideas in this book are not mine. They are my humble attempt to express the Torah wisdom of my teachers. Much of my thinking has been shaped by the work of Rabbi David Aaron, Rebbetzin Tziporah Heller, Rabbi Leib Kelemen, Miriam Kosman, Rabbi Lord Jonathan Sacks, Rabbi Akiva Tatz, and Rabbi Shlomo Wolbe, *zt"l*. I pray that my expression of their Torah reflects the truth of their teachings.

To my teachers, I thank you for opening the door to wisdom. Thank you to Rabbi Ahron Hoch, Rabbi Tzvi Sytner, Reb Zale Newman, Abi Samole, Esther Taub, and David Grant, for your support, invaluable belief in this project, and the opportunity to grow as a member of the Village Shul community. To Lou Orzech, *a"h*, who opened the door to partnering with the Village Shul and who always believed in the "choosing up" message. I miss your smiling face in my classes. To Rabbi Posen, whose Torah, guidance, and encouragement have been invaluable. To my Uncle Elliott, Rabbi Diamond, for teaching me how to listen carefully to questions and see the messages of Chazal. To Adrienne Gold Davis, for your mentorship, absolute honesty, and encouragement to "be no one other than myself." To Susan Zehavi, for pushing me to "take a trip I had no time for" and making sure I went on this journey. To

Rav Yosef Weissman, for taking the risk as our teacher and your deep commitment to our growth, one micro-*avodah* at a time. To Rabbi Leib Kelemen, for guiding my growth and investing the time to review and comment on the manuscript.

To Lori Palatnik, for your vision, invaluable comments on the manuscript, and for founding a movement where each woman can find her way to change the world. To the women I have taken on trips, for being along this spiritual journey together with me. To my "Big Shves," for leading the way. To Rabbi Joel Wardinger, the Yorkville Jewish Centre, and Olami, for providing me the space and support to grow a young women's Torah learning program.

To the ladies of my classes — learning and growing with you is truly the highlight of my week, the space where I feel "it's not just me," and where we all find the permission to grow using Torah as our guide. Thank you.

To the Village Shul community, for being "my people and my place."

To Kim Smiley, for your support, collaboration, and comments. Let's see where the next chapter takes us.

To Rebbetzin Dini Coopersmith, for your belief and help with this project. To Rebbetzin Tziporah Heller and Rabbi Paysach Krohn, for taking the time to read and comment on the manuscript. Your time is precious, and I am indebted to you for your contribution.

To Rabbi Nechemia Coopersmith and Aish.com, for publishing pieces that encouraged me to share more authentically.

To Rabbi Doron Kornbluth and the dedicated staff of Mosaica Press, for believing in this book, your support throughout the process, and making this dream a reality.

To my fearless editor Aharona Gans, for your tireless efforts, fierce friendship, and heartful editing. Thank you for taking on the task of wrangling my "creative grammar" and challenging me to discover what I really mean.

To the WaterStone Clinic crew, you were the place I landed for many of the days I was finding my way. To Dr. Stephanie Bot, for opening the door to the next chapter and allowing a deeper connection between my spiritual path and my work as a psychotherapist.

To the readers of my weekly email — your feedback and encouragement keep me going. I write knowing that the words are received with kind eyes, open hearts, and listening souls. Thank you.

To M.W. and P.W., for making the space for me to accept and discover my story.

To my *mishpachah*, you are a source of ongoing *berachah* and teach me what it is to *be* a *berachah*. To my grandparents, who would have *shepped* so much *nachas* and to whom I pray to bring *nachas*.

To my sisters, Sarah and Darya, and my brother-in-law, Omri — you are the people who get me. Your unwavering support, feedback, love, and cheerleading keeps me going. I hope I can give to you what you have gifted to me.

To Shevi, for filling my life with wonder and whose idea for a book title, "Text Messages to Hashem," continues to inspire me. I am so proud to be your mother.

To Marc, for finding me at just the right time. Your kindness and depth of commitment to Torah, growth, and truth inspire me each day. May we merit to build together.

To my parents, there are no words. You have never stopped believing in me. The lessons and values you have planted for your children are a testament to your humble greatness. May we bring you much *berachah*.

And above all, to Hashem, my Creator and Sustainer, "From the depths I called out to You, from expansiveness You have answered me." I pray that this book and my life serve as the vessel for Your vision.

And to you, my dear reader. We are in this together. Let's begin.

**Choosing up** \'chü-ziŋ 'əp\: *The moment-to-moment practice of seeking meaning, opportunities for growth, and G-d in our experiences. Making deliberate choices about how we think, speak, and act to elevate the everyday.*

**Examples:**

*// We are choosing up by being kind to strangers this week.*

*// I had a hard day but chose up when I saw G-d was with me in the struggle.*

*// She chooses up by being patient in that challenging relationship.*

# Introduction

I have always been captivated by stories. Hearing them. Telling them. Creating them in the quiet spaces of my mind. Stories provide an escape to adventure and endless possibility. Stories carry us across time and space. But the most powerful element of stories is that they can carry us home—to ourselves, bringing us clarity in our experiences and personal purpose. This is why stories can move us so deeply and profoundly. We have an Aha! moment when we recognize ourselves in someone else's story.

Storytelling isn't simply for entertainment. It is a powerful tool for transmitting values and guidance. The Torah uses stories to instruct us on how to live our lives. The narrative of our ancestors reveals the struggles of being human and the strength of our soul to persevere and grow. The power of the story is not confined to Torah figures. It is ours as well. How do we co-write with G-d the stories of our lives?

This question has troubled me as much as it has inspired me. Like most, I had a dream for my life and then there was, of course, what *actually* happened. Like all, I have experienced ups and downs: Great family/schoolyard bullies. Amazing friends/internal angst. Spiritual path/health challenges. In each circumstance, I have tried to find meaning in what felt like messiness.

I found that the stories I tell myself affect the way I feel and act. If the narrator in my head is hopeful, the world is filled with light and I'm up for any challenge. If she's counting everything that's wrong with reality, the world is flooded with darkness and it's hard to put one foot in front of the other.

It's not just me. This phenomenon is borne out in the psychological research as much as in my own experience. Storytelling can make or break us. So why don't we just tell nice stories and then everything will be good? Not so easy. It's one thing to tell hopeful tales when things are going well; it's quite another when life sends us unexpected plot twists and disappointments. What can we do when our story seems to break down?

One of my "major story breakdowns" came with a divorce within months of my daughter's birth. It wasn't just my life plot that felt broken; *I* felt broken. I was forced to look at my story as it *was*, shattered dreams and all, and to *begin* telling my story anew. It was a slow process. It was with lots of support. It was not glamorous. And yes, it was *a lot* of storytelling. Sometimes life, like a good story, needs lots of editing, rewriting, and reimagining.

As I write this, it has been over a decade of digging through the rubble and the messiness of my life to find gems made of meaning in my daily experiences. These have helped me reconstruct my dreams and rebuild my relationship with G-d, others, and the core of my being. And the journey is ongoing.

The more I dig, the more gems I find, giving me the courage to continue sifting through my days for the lessons that G-d wants me to learn. In fact, this is really the theme of every person's life story: finding the courage to keep learning and growing. This is our "soul mission," which I refer to throughout the book.

I remember the fateful day a few years ago, when I excitedly sat down at my kitchen table to write the first of what would turn out to be a weekly email that would gradually grow in readership and become the basis for this book, *Choosing Up*.

I had just returned from Israel, where I led a women's mission with the Jewish Women's Renaissance Project. I had been dreaming of writing daily anecdotes as a "that-would-be-nice-to-do-one-day" sort of idea, and now I had a small group of women with whom I had bonded deeply; I saw these relationships as the perfect audience for sharing my search for meaning in the everyday.

What began as an exercise in sharing became a sort of soul therapy for me. Even if I thought I had nothing to write, I would feel compelled to sit down at my laptop and inevitably, a story from my week would emerge. Through the exercise of seeking out daily gems, the world has become illuminated in new ways, and I have discovered G-d and meaning in even the darkest of places. My life has been changed. I believe we all can access this way of living. We all have a story. We all have a choice in how we tell it. Each moment is a new opportunity.

*Choosing Up* is intended to be used as a tool and can be read and applied in many ways. This book is a practice in finding stories of hope with the purpose of bringing more wholeness to our lives and to the world. You can read it alone or in groups. You can use the book as a platform for discussion or as a template to write your own stories. Maybe you'll choose to share them. *Choosing Up* could become a community, a movement, or a way of life. The story is still unfolding...

# CHAPTER 1
# Choice

"Between stimulus and response there is a space. In that space is our power to choose our response. In our response lies our growth and freedom."

(Viktor Frankl)

*"Rabbi Yehudah says: The entire world stood on one side, and Avraham stood on the other side."*

*(Midrash Rabbah, Bereishis 42:8)*

You don't have to be a marathon runner to understand the magic of Mile 13. Let me explain.

There is a point in the course (of any race with a half and a full marathon) where there is a turn off, aka Mile 13. Continue to the right, and you have another 13.2 miles ahead. Mazel tov, you signed up for a full marathon: 26.2 miles. Veer to the left, and you are 0.1 miles away from cheering crowds and a finish line. That's the way I go—13.1 miles is quite enough for me.

Each time, I look at the full-marathoners and think, *No thank you. I'm done.* Now, some of you might be thinking, *Are you insane? There's no way I'd sign up for either.* Fair enough. But let me ask you, how many times a day do we decide which way we want to go? To be honest, I am never tempted to continue with the full-marathon runners. But there are some people who, after completing the half, have only one goal in mind: train so that next time they veer to the right. Beautiful. Just not my thing. It's easy to say, because no one's feelings are in the mix. I'm not worried I'll offend if I choose a different course. I'll be in good company. That makes either choice a little easier. But the real magic of Mile 13 is the moment when we realize: I have to choose a route—independent of where others are headed. In fact, I might have to go alone. But the choice is mine to make and I can't be swayed by the crowd.

Deciding on a running route is not the biggest deal, I concede. Life doesn't hinge on a race course. But it does rely on each of us making choices and standing our ground. And that requires drawing some lines in the sand.

Speaking the truth about who we are and what we believe is not always easy. When we stand up and set boundaries, we risk disappointing or offending. Are you thinking half-marathoning is appealing at this point? A few hard hours are nothing compared to the daily tests we face. When we're scared of letting people down, being judged, or facing confrontation, we may be tempted to just "go with the flow." Sometimes that is the right thing to do. But what about the moments when the "flow" isn't right? When the flow doesn't match up with our values? When the world at large doesn't fit with who we are? That's when the magic of Mile 13 comes in—where we find the courage to follow our path and claim our decisions.

We can't and won't be able to make everyone happy. Living hostage to others' approval will rob us of ourselves. And that, my friends, is a dangerous path. If we are too scared of rejection and too concerned with pleasing others, we will never discover who we really are. If we try to run in both the full and the half marathon at once, we won't finish either one. If we try to be everything to everyone, we'll be no one at all.

A woman once told me, "I might not agree with everything you do, your lifestyle, and choices. But I respect your conviction. It's given me permission to take a stand in my own life, with my family." She taught me so much. It takes courage to stand on one side while the rest of the world stands on the other. This is not about shaking fists or seeking conflict. It is about standing with certainty in our values, the willingness to assert, "This is what I believe," despite what people might say. It takes grace and decisiveness. We won't make everyone happy—but we win respect when we live our values and are people of integrity.

This business of choice making comes with a risk: we won't always get it right. We require teachers, people who will help us make these calls and give us feedback. We will need to know when to concede and apologize for poor decisions. That's part of the course. It builds our choice making muscles; it keeps us humble along the path.

You may not be a runner. You may never run a full or a half marathon. But you also face multiple turnoffs, difficult choices, and times when you are called to take a stand. If you look carefully throughout your day, you too will see that magical turn off at Mile 13.

There are some moments that seem as if they are happening in slow motion. They are rarely the times we wish would linger. Achingly long afternoons, drawn-out nights, or times we see something falling, as it happens. As was the case on a Friday afternoon. I was on edge. Making my way around the kitchen, I couldn't help but notice my inner critic in good form—in addition to being irritated, I was berating myself for being in a bad mood.

"I'm sorry, I'm a little bit more cranky than usual today," I said to my daughter. I guess the hope was that by naming and admitting my struggle, I would somehow tame the tired and snappy beast within. I continued, "Anyway, I just wanted to say that. I'm trying my best." What I've edited out so far was that all of this was relayed as I tried to tidy, prep food, and make myself a coffee. This is where the slow-motion effect starts.

The echo of my words, "trying my best," lingered in the air as I reached for my freshly made coffee. Somewhere between extending my hand and grasping that cup, the reel comes to a near halt. You see it unfolding. Frazzled woman mid-afternoon, almost making it to that hot java. Until she doesn't. Cup drops. Coffee splashes. Everywhere. Floor, counter, and everything in between. Then it shifts out of slow motion, and in a split-second the film is once again moving at high speed, as is the narrow window of reaction time.

I suppose the test of saying that we're trying our best is when we're given the chance to prove it. I looked over at the witness to my coffee fumble. Scrambling for towels, taking in a deep breath, I remarked, "I guess this is today's test."

As my daughter and I mopped, cleaned, and muttered, I began to narrate the play-by-play. "And Mommy swoops in with paper towels, daughter assists with extra rags. Coffee is dribbling down the counter, but ladies and gentlemen, we won't be discouraged." We started to laugh. Even as I discovered untold surfaces of coffee puddles, I kept up the running commentary. We giggled at the absurdity of it all. Somehow, putting words to the incident and externalizing the struggle shifted the experience. We became co-conspirators in our reaction, forming a new narrative. Notice, I didn't say we created a story we loved or were excited about. I'd rather not have spent that time mopping up the coffee I was craving. But isn't that how it goes with most of the messy moments in life?

We can't avoid stress and heartbreak, but we *can* choose the story we tell about it. "I am always stressed" can become, "I am feeling stressed right now." Instead of saying, "Bad things always happen to me," we can reflect, "I have had a lot of pain, I am learning to live with my challenges."

These tiny tweaks can have a large effect. Shifting our language changes how we relate to ourselves and the world. By noting that we *feel* stressed instead of we *are* stressed, we acknowledge that there is more to us than the emotion or struggle of the moment. We may not believe it, but our words will point us in that direction. By naming our feelings, we begin to process and overcome adversity.

A few slips and spills along the road (or in the kitchen) are downright inevitable. What is not automatic is how we choose to experience and tell the story. Embedded in every proclamation that "I'm doing my best" is the chance to, well, just keep on trying our best. This usually means calling upon our inner narrator and carefully deciding what we want our next sentences to accomplish.

When I described the coffee spill out loud, it sounded pretty funny. We laughed. We lightened up. It became easier to "try my best." I am always a little wary of sharing these sorts of blunders. My feeling is that when I do so, the Almighty, in His infinite love, keeps me honest and ensures that I have ample opportunity to practice these written words in my life.

So, I will not be surprised if I keep spilling things. Or at least find myself mopping up some life-size messes in my days. But maybe this time I'll remember: it was from the difficult moment itself that my inner tension melted. Had I not endured that spill, I would not have seen the power of my words to shift my reality. And for that, I am grateful.

Maybe next time we find ourselves grumbling over life-plans-gone-awry and everyday spills, we'll take the chance to tell a new story.

*"The whole world is a very narrow bridge, and the main thing to recall is to not make ourselves afraid."*

(Rebbe Nachman of Breslov)

I have discovered a new pastime, a spontaneous hobby. OK, calling it a hobby may be pushing it, but it's definitely in the category of simple everyday pleasures.

It happened as the umpteenth promotional email of the day arrived in my inbox: I discovered something.

There I was, opening up one of those emails with the intent of deleting it right away, when I wondered, *How did I end up on this list?* There are some I recall signing up for, but a flurry of other promotional emails somehow, surreptitiously, find their way to my inbox.

I paused further, cursor hovering over *delete*…and then I realized, I had another option. Not to delete. But rather scroll all the way to the bottom—and choose to *unsubscribe*. And just like that, voilà, I did it! I have taken to reliving this pleasure on several occasions. Within a couple of clicks, I became a bit of an unsubscribe junky.

If only it could be as simple as a couple of clicks to let go of the other stuff we'd rather not hold on to. Imagine driving to work or washing the dishes, and a thought, a fear, a nagging voice invades your reality. Suddenly you're wrapped up in worry, no longer present in your day. You wish you could get back to that pre-busy-mind place, but it's too late. Imagine scrolling to the bottom of your mind, clicking *unsubscribe*, and returning to serenity! A few steps, and you'd be unhooked from the mental chatter that drains your soul and disconnects you from your purpose.

Not. So. Simple.

Yet, the email universe does have some wisdom for us: we too can stop, slow down, and scroll to the bottom.

When we see more of the picture—of our lives and our focus—we can begin to actively choose how we spend our time and where we direct our attention. When we simply try to delete emails, thoughts, or struggles, they keep coming back. Building a wall against thoughts and emotions has a way of keeping them in. Instead, we can pause long enough to really listen to the stories we are telling ourselves. The ones that include lines like, "I will never...," "Why does this always...," or "If that happens, I can't...," offer us the opportunity to ask ourselves, "How do I *make* myself afraid? What are the lines I feed my mind that leave me discouraged?"

When we see what we are holding on to, we can likewise look at what no longer serves us. It's not about destroying those parts—it's rather the art of gently letting go. We don't need to hold on so tight. Not every thought that comes our way deserves a spot in our soul. That's the beauty of unsubscribing. When we learn to let go, we make room to focus on the beauty and connection available in each moment.

Deleting is wishing the thought out of existence; unsubscribing is releasing it, gently loosening our minds' grip on a belief. Instead of telling ourselves, "I shouldn't be scared, I should stop worrying about that," we can speak kindly to ourselves: "It makes sense you are fearful. How is that voice inside trying to protect you? Is it doing its job? Would you like to let go of it, even for a bit?" Sometimes we unsubscribe by sharing with a friend, other times we can turn to G-d: "Hashem, this is what is worrying me, this is what I am so scared of. I want to give a piece of it to You. Help me let go of this fear." We may still worry at times, but we will see that we are not our worries. Fear may pass through our minds, but it need not define us. With this new freedom, we can redirect our attention back to joy, hope, and Hashem.

As I said, I have discovered a new pastime when it comes to unsubscribing. It's not a one-time event, rather, a daily practice of sorting through my inbox. Our spiritual work is also an ongoing process. When we see the active role that we are taking in cultivating fear—entertaining obsessive thoughts and worries like they are guests—then it becomes a choice: hold on tight or try unsubscribing. Each time we notice our scared selves emerging, it's an opportunity to practice the art of letting go. So, next time you notice worry brain kicking in, no need to get upset—it's just a chance to practice a new pastime.

The sign at the gas station pump read, "Cash Only. Please Pay Inside." I hesitated for a moment. In the second between, *Who carries cash these days?* and, *Oh yes, I have some*, the conversation in my head went from annoyed to relief, all in a gas-pump-moment. Having regained my refueling composure, I filled the tank and entered to pay.

All was going according to plan B. Handing over my payment, I commented on the "Cash Only. No Debit or Credit," sign propped up by the cashier. "Yes," he sighed. "All the stations across the province are cash only. A computer glitch."

I offered an empathetic sigh and smile as I paid. He commented that some customers had yelled at him in frustration, as if the cause for this inconvenience was in his hands. We marveled together at the absurdity of thinking that yelling at a gas station attendant would get anyone closer to their goal. As I made my way toward the door he quipped, "Someone high up is gonna get it for this one."

His words trailed in my mind as I drove away. I admit that I had judged the kind of customer he described, thinking that (regardless of the veracity of the thought), "I would never do that." I marveled at the silliness of "shooting the messenger." Yet, the idea that someone was responsible held appeal; there was relief in knowing there was a place to point a finger.

It is so tempting to be pulled into the blame game. If I can find the person who made this all go wrong, then I can...do what? Yell? Scream? Tell them to fix it, change themselves or the situation? Of course, there is a point to seeing where and how an error occurred, and addressing the players involved. But there is something deceptively delicious about finding that singular "higher up person," as if he or she absolves us of the one thing for which we remain responsible: *ourselves*.

No matter what, I couldn't have fixed the gas station's "cash only" problem. And even if we could find the one who made the error, what then? The trap that lies in thinking someone out there bears all the blame is that it excludes us from the solution. My gas station management skills may be lacking—but my ability to choose my next move and how I act when I'm challenged belongs to me alone. The only real choice we have is how we react in each and every moment in time.

It's easy to point fingers and expect other people to build us up and define our lives. Friends can help. Mentors will guide. But ultimately, we are accountable for the choices we make and the paths we pursue. It's not on the shoulders of someone "higher up," or even my Creator. It's on me. It is what makes us human. It's the gift of free will.

Using our free will to choose a life of meaning means checking out the illusions that trap us. We may believe, *I could grow, if only I had a different life*. We may think, *If only I had different parents, then I could heal*. We may even blame the gas station attendant for our bad mood. In truth, G-d sent us those parents, this life, and yes, that gas station. What remains within our control is the degree to which we build a relationship with Hashem. When the details of our life become hints of the Divine, our choices change—we see our power in defining our responses. The organizing question of our life becomes: *Who can I become in this circumstance?* And *that* is an answer worth finding.

*"Everyone has a unique path waiting for them to journey on."*

*(Rabbi David Aaron)*[1]

From my view running along the path, something seemed amiss. A figure up ahead was half bent over toward one side. Though I was keeping a steady pace, I was ready to stop and see if help was needed. Drawing closer, the scenario shifted. I saw a woman turning in my direction and motioning to be quiet. Finger to lips, she pointed to the other side of the path. There in the bushes was a little brown bunny rabbit. I crouched at the woman's side, watching our little friend, who didn't budge, though we were only a couple feet away. Another runner came up behind who likewise stopped to admire this fuzzy creature. There was something uniting about our shared wonder. In a sense, we were all beholden to the bunny—waiting for him to make the first move. I began to wonder how long it would be before we could move on. That is, until a third runner approached. The self-appointed bunny traffic controller launched into her now well-rehearsed directions, motioning him to stop.

But get this: the runner slowed, he watched, *but he did not stop*. In fact, he trotted right by. And even more, that bunny didn't move an inch. A pretty radical move for the runner when the crowd was frozen in observation. Runner #3 had broken the status quo, he didn't need to stop just because that's what was "being done."

The third runner gave the rest of us permission—we could move on. Yes, the bunny was indeed a delight. I'm the first to marvel at everyday wonders and revel in such a shared experience. What struck me most was the way reality shifted when runner #3 chose to act differently. It expanded the choices available to the rest of us. Our well-meaning traffic controller did not have the corner on reality. There were (literally) multiple paths available. I'm not saying we shouldn't have stopped. What I am suggesting is that the stopping did not preclude restarting or choosing a new pace and destination.

When we are part of a group, we can fall into patterns of behavior

---

1    *The Secret Life of God: Discovering the Divine within You* (Boston and London: Shambhala, 2004).

without even noticing. We do "what's done" without understanding the rationale for those choices or even realizing our power to choose. We need to belong to a community, joining in shared values and actions; but within that framework we are charged to define our personal path. No one can do that for us. When we let others decide for us, we abdicate the most precious gift G-d has given us: the power to choose.

I'm not sure who had the starring role on the path that morning: the bunny, the traffic-stopper, the runner, or me. Maybe all of us, but in different ways. We each held a different piece of reality. We all had our own perspective. More important than the role we played was the choice we all made. In deciding how to respond, we clarified a little bit about who we each were and our personal path. We are not in this world to simply stop because someone says so. Nor are we meant to go just because we're told we can.

In forging our spiritual paths, we are enjoined to slow, sometimes even pause, all the while searching for understanding. We will not always comprehend with our limited intellect the rationale behind any given life-stopping moment. But it doesn't free us from trying, from looking at every moment in our day as a chance to make a choice, an opportunity to find our path.

We ask for wisdom. We recognize that we don't accomplish this alone. It takes mentors, guides, and G-d's assistance. But sometimes, between the everyday challenges and bunny rabbit delights, we find a little bit of the, "That's why it happened," or, "This is my next step." Stumbling upon understanding and clarifying our choices, like roadside rabbit watching, doesn't happen by accident. It's the product of constantly searching for insight and keeping our eyes open. Then we can exercise our Divine gift—and make a choice.

Why is it that getting through the mountain of laundry looks more daunting than scaling Kilimanjaro? Or making it through another hour of waiting seems harder than making it to a marathon finish line?

Sometimes, it takes heroic measures to survive another gray afternoon. These days are usually accompanied by an internal script that chants, "This is too much, how can I go on?"

You may not be feeling overwhelmed today. You might have a calm sense of determination as you face the piles of bills and laundry.

Yet hiding right around the corner, lurking in the crevices of determination, is a little voice that waits to pounce—to plant seeds of doubt and make us question ourselves. It creeps up when we are tired; it preys on our unique vulnerabilities.

That voice in your head might use different words or imagery, but you know its telltale tone. And while it is clear that the analogy of mountainous housework the likes of Mount Everest is, well, just an analogy, it begs the question: Why do we have days when all seems possible and others when we can't seem to make it past our front door?

We tend to believe that what we think and feel *is* reality. In truth, our thoughts and feelings are not facts. They provide useful data, they can be our guides, but they can equally lead us down dark paths away from our purpose. It's not always possible to "feel better" or "think more positively." Rather, our mission is to become more mindful feelers and thinkers. We do this by building an awareness of our thoughts and emotions. When we slow down long enough to notice what is going on inside, we can begin to make choices about where we put our attention. By slowing down and tuning in to our internal experience, we become less reactive and more intentional about what we do with the voices chanting, "I can't cope!"

We might start by noticing, *Hey, when I check my email, I'm flooded with anxiety,* or, *Huh, each time I visit that place I start berating myself.* With this slight shift, we drive a tiny wedge between ourselves and our reactions—and in that space, we open up a world of possibility, where we can choose how we respond to our circumstances. We can start deciding where to focus and find new ways of viewing our experiences.

Shifting our perspective is not just a matter of repackaging our lives—as in new wrapping, same issues. Problems cannot be tied up in bows. So, what then *is* the power of perspective? When we see things from a new viewpoint, we don't change the landscape, we change *ourselves.* We become the kind of people who can make choices about how we live and where we focus. The change is not about the outside world, it's about how we encounter our inner experience. The more we practice perspective shifting, the more possibilities we discover—in how we want to act and who we want to become.

We may never unlock the secret of why one day feels OK and another, with the seemingly same set of perks and challenges, has us flooded with doubt. But we may find the ability to look at the mountains—made of jagged rock, or socks and T-shirts—and see where we can choose to look and how we will react. It requires stopping long enough to realize: *My experience is only part of the picture. There are other ways to see this, there are possibilities beyond me, there is more to this world than I know.* And sometimes, that's all we need to shift and make our way over that mountain to the next day.

*"Turning feelings into words can help us process and overcome adversity."*

*(Sheryl Sandberg and Adam Grant)[2]*

Listening to and telling stories about my grandmother at her shivah, I came to know new parts of who she was. In the telling itself, I discovered pieces of her I had once known but had forgotten. I have memories of selecting sweets from her tiered candy dish, and the lilt of her voice as she left her ever long-winded messages on my voice mail. While she won't be calling again, these memories feel like she is leaving one last message for me. There are stories that reveal different sides of my grandmother, and I feel myself getting to know her better. They are affirmations of a woman with whom I spent many an ice-cream-filled afternoon.

Her pearls of wisdom and seemingly simple reflections on life peppered our time together, and she had a unique way of spinning a tale

---

2    *Option B: Facing Adversity, Building Resilience, and Finding Joy* (New York: Alfred A. Knopf, 2017).

to create a positive perspective. The way she translated her experiences into a narrative of hope and contentment enabled her to find peace with her life. How do you convey a person's essence? Stories, like Hansel and Gretel's crumbs, can leave hints that trace the journey of who and what a person was...but cannot quite capture the essence of the soul itself. However, in the silences, in the gaps between who she was and what she has left behind for us to learn, is the promise of knowing her more deeply.

Stories are an essential tool of communication; they can inspire, linking us to a rich history and a possible future. They can likewise be the internal narrative that drags us into fear and hopelessness. When we tell ourselves over and over that we can't and we won't, that we "know how this goes," and create one bleak story line, we shut the door on connection, growth, and new possibility.

I found a video of my grandmother taken a few years ago. It was the week after she sat shivah for my grandfather. She is playing basketball with my then four-year-old daughter. "Now your turn to throw the ball," she coaches. When her great-granddaughter makes the shot, she lets out a holler of glee. She is in the game; she is in pure delight. As much as her mourning is fresh, she is in touch with the remaining joy and opportunity in her life.

When we include hope in the story we tell about ourselves—even if laced with pain, darkness, or fear—we make room for new possibilities. The up-and-down cycle of the days, months, and years can hold us hostage or set us free. We have the ability to choose how we narrate our experiences and who we seek as our listeners. Will we repeat over and over how hard and stressful everything is and how much we are struggling? Or will we relate how we are managing, even thriving, under stress and find reasons to celebrate our micro-successes and voice our gratitude? Our primary (and likely most important) audience will always be ourselves. Do we speak kindly to ourselves, naming our courage and resilience? Or do we chastise and berate?

The people we touch and our everyday actions are the bread crumbs that we leave along our paths—clues to who we are and how we live. Listening to anecdotes about my grandmother helped me trace the arc of her life; it also helped me look at my own life. The thrilling thing about sharing our narrative is that we have some influence over the storyline. We can't control most of the plot, but we can decide what twist to put on the chapter we are living and how we make sense of our challenges.

My grandmother lived a difficult life. She never denied her struggle—but when she related her experiences, it was always with a sense of wonder and a touch of humor. I miss her. I'm hoping I won't miss the gift she left behind for us all: the power to shape our story.

**"Who is powerful? He who controls his passions."**

*(Pirkei Avos 4:1)*

I sent a friend an email a couple of weeks ago, just touching base. No reply. Then I forgot about it. Life gets busy. Emails go unopened, unanswered. It happens. Then, a surprise arrived in my inbox—her reply.

"Things are super hectic these days and I can't seem to find any time to reply to my emails." I got it. Hectic is my middle name. I replied: "Maybe one day…when you take a breath, I'll get a chance to hear about everything that you are fabulously busy with!"

Fabulously busy. Accomplishing. Doing great things. Ah, sounds good, doesn't it? The stuff that makes headlines in the marquis of life. In response, she wrote: "Don't get your hopes too high. Mountains of laundry to wash and fold, sinks of dishes to wash, messes to tidy, groceries to buy, meals to prepare…that's what keeps me running on the hamster wheel these days. Nothing life-altering."

The daily grind, one foot in front of the other. In darkness. In light. Slogging through when there is no applause or cheering squad shouting, "Good work! Job well done!" The private moments of building a life. Decidedly unglamorous. And so, we write them off as "nothing life altering," but we miss out if we dismiss them as unimportant; it's how we show up in those everyday tasks that can have the greatest impact on who we become.

It is in the micro-moments of our lives where we become great. Each little struggle we conquer builds our capacity to face the bigger stuff. When we exercise a bit of patience or give a little smile, we are building our spiritual muscles. It's when we rise to the occasion in these "little moments" that we have strength for the "big times" in life.

Ask any Olympic athlete: more important than race day are the hours of practice clocked when no one is looking. We will likewise be defined by who we are in the privacy of our homes. We want to have a melt-down, but we keep our cool. We could eat the entire cake, but we stop after a piece. Exercising self-control is the birthplace of personal power. True power is not about lording over others, it's about how we deal with ourselves.

Still, it's tough to value the everyday as "powerful" and "great." How many times, after biting your tongue instead of snapping back in anger, have you picked up the phone to report that nanosecond of self-control? When, after getting groceries at the end of a long day, did you post "bought milk instead of having a breakdown"? Or what about that day, when nothing was going your way, and all you wanted to do was give in to a fit of chocolate, anger, wine, or righteous indignation, and instead you took a deep breath and a long bath? *That* is medal-worthy conduct. In a world that devalues private spaces and personal victories, we need to reclaim our power.

We can mistake the seemingly mundane for unimportant. We think that choosing kindness in moments of stress, managing another day when we are exhausted, is nothing to report. But those are the choices that define us. The greatest battle is inside each of us. And therefore, the biggest victory is in facing ourselves.

In my friend's email, she described herself as "super hectic." When I asked her what she meant, she recounted her daily tasks and described them as "nothing life altering." I challenged her on that point: those *are* the life-altering moments. I challenge us all to look a little differently at our lives and reclaim our power.

─────────────── YOUR TURN: GUIDE QUESTIONS ───────────────

- When do you struggle to live according to your values? How can you make a small choice today to live more in line with who you want to be?
- Where is it hard to see the good in your life? What statement can you use in times of stress to help you focus on the positive?
- What is a story you tell yourself about your life? Is it helping you? Do you want to choose to tell it differently? Try it out for today.
- Who are your guides and mentors? Can you make some time today to connect to someone who helps you grow spiritually and connects you to Torah?

# CHAPTER 2

# Resilience

"The righteous one falls seven times and arises."
(*Mishlei* 24:16)

I pulled out of a parking spot—or rather made several attempts at doing so. It was between the curb and street that I once again encountered my own imperfection. I had pulled into a narrow spot in one of the parking lots designed with all tight angles, high curbs, and strange alignments—some urban planner's idea of a practical joke. Getting in was no problem. But when it came time to reverse, I had an audience of drivers all waiting for me as I tried, and tried again, to extricate myself from this concrete labyrinth. I was *that* driver. With a commentary of criticism in my head and a row of cars behind me, I tried to stay calm. It must have been just a few moments, but it felt like an eternity—a slow-motion exercise in humility.

Not getting it right on the first, fifth, or fiftieth attempt has a way of breaking us down. Believing we ought to have done better can subtly sap us of our strength and our will to move forward.

"How come you're here again?" and "Why do you always mess this up?" are familiar chants of self-reproach. These little voices come to haunt us when we believe we should have done or known better.

If they were reserved for backing out of tight spots, we'd be doing OK. It's when we constantly hold the measuring stick of perfection up to ourselves that we get into trouble. Believing that mistakes are a sign of weakness makes failure into the enemy. We will do almost anything to avoid it. But what if we could see that the purpose was never about getting it perfect? What if needing to regroup and retry was wired right into the plan?

Our work is not to avoid the blunders of being human; it is choosing to learn from them. Like a revolving door in our lives, we get to re-believe in ourselves over and over again. This isn't easy. We have grown up in a world that values high marks and shiny successes. There is nothing glamorous about a mistake, no applause for our failures. Confronted with our shortcomings, we tend to feel insecure and hide, worrying that we'll be rejected for our faults. But what if there was another way to feel about mistake making? What if we welcomed each foible as an opportunity?

Every time we fail, each moment we see where we missed the mark, we get to choose—to hope we can be done with making mistakes once and for all, or to whisper back to ourselves, "I trust you. You can learn from this."

We are not defined by our mistakes, we are defined by how we react. The art of readjusting, like any skill set, is learned through practice. No one gets into a car and automatically knows how to drive…or park. We learn through doing.

When the world is watching our mini (or massive) missteps—we can hide in shame or we can show up with courage. It takes strength to say, "Yes, I didn't get it right. Now let's see how I can do better."

How would your life be different if the next time you snapped at your kid or bombed a project at work, you said to yourself, "OK, I'm human, now what?"

I made it back on the road that day, and I (mostly) made it past my embarrassment. It's one thing with a parking spot; it's another with the more serious ways we falter. But I believe that the approach is the same—a willingness to see ourselves as error artists, constantly in the pursuit of learning from our mess ups.

When we aren't afraid of getting it wrong, we're more willing to take risks, try new things, and persevere in the face of obstacles. When mistakes become openings, we stop hiding and start showing up.

We have the power to create a culture of permission—to be human, to make mistakes, and to keep trying. It starts with how we talk to ourselves and what we choose to reveal to each other. What would it be like if you weren't afraid to tell your boss that you fumbled? How can you make your kids less afraid to admit they did something wrong? Learning from our failings is not a one-time event; it is a way of being. It is a commitment to forgiving ourselves and each other for being imperfect. Only once we embrace our humanity can we begin to grow and do better.

Maybe next time you see *that* driver struggling with a spot, or start to berate yourself, you'll pause and remember that it's not about avoiding the mistake, it's about finding the courage to keep trying.

**"Who makes the wind blow and makes the rain descend."**

**(Amidah prayer)**

I like the autumn. Fall colors lining the streets. Shorter days. Raking. Crunchy leaves under foot. It all sounds romantic. While I like the colors—as well as scarves and fall boots—it is with a definite sense of sadness and resignation that I let go of summer and surrender to fall. I'm a summer girl at heart.

Nevertheless, I appreciate seasons and the way they punctuate the year. Weather—winter, spring, summer, or fall—we love it or hate it. We talk about it in the elevator, by the water cooler, in line at the grocery store. We are obsessed with the weather. So, what is it about the changing of the seasons that we take so to heart? Perhaps it's the change itself. The knowledge that nothing, not even the air we breathe or the trees that line our street, is stable. None of it is static. Yet, there is a force behind each shift we experience. G-d is making that wind blow and those drops of rain descend. To feel this, to see His Hand in our life, is to sense our utter reliance on our Creator.

With all our effort to micromanage and control reality, feeling our essential dependence can be jarring. There is seemingly a way to plan and anticipate most things in life. We buy organizing systems, upgrade devices, and check off to-do lists, all in the name of improved efficiency. But the fact remains: however much we may *think* we are building and becoming smarter, the seasons still turn, the weather comes and goes, and we have little say in the matter, other than tuning into the radio and grabbing an umbrella. The only thing we can count on staying the same is change itself.

I'm not just talking about physical changes, like the colors of the leaves or the tires on your car. Because just when you think you have it figured out—workplace politics and bedtime routines—who you are and where you are going can change.

That's the point. Our job is not to maintain a static reality where we can micromanage every moment. Believe me, I've tried. Instead, it's about how we weather each storm that makes us wonder why it's raining on our parade. Can we practice looking at each drop of rain, joy, and aggravation as an opportunity to stretch and grow?

When we stop long enough to notice the changes happening around us, we find room in our internal landscape to shift as well. Here's the thing: it's all about movement, the willingness to adapt and grow as we are challenged. The most stable structures are those that can bend in the wind. Flexibility allows for resilience; it means that we can stretch and move with the pressures of life. In contrast, rigidity, in both the physical and spiritual realm, leaves us fragile and less able to adapt.

When we see the changes of life as *part* of the journey, instead of an impediment, we shed the need to resist the process. What if we could tell ourselves that as surely as the Almighty controls the weather, He is likewise sending these challenges just for me? They are the Divine curriculum of my soul. Each pressure is a chance to bend in the wind, to build my resilience and trust in the process.

Change will come, and we will want to dig in our heels and resist. That's OK; we need not stay there. For with the same certainty of seasons changing comes another promise—we can learn to be flexible, we can cultivate resilience. It all starts with change. G-d will keep sending change our way; our choice is how we react to each challenge. The secret, as the leaves might tell us, is accepting the Almighty's invitation to grow with the seasons.

I watched the scene unfold across the playground: kid on bike, kid off bike, kid crying. Mom was soon by her side. Knees and hands were inspected. Tears wiped away. Kid cajoled back onto the bike, a few more loops around the bike path and once again, she was off her bike. Mom looked like she was trying to get her back on, but the kid wouldn't budge. The pair walked the bike over to a bench, sitting down within earshot.

"I don't want to keep riding. I don't want to fall off." Fair enough. Given that I wasn't the parent with an agenda in this scenario, I thought the kid made a good point.

"But you were doing such a great job," the mom soothed.

"But then I fell!" The little girl's voice quivered, clearly on the edge of tears. I could almost hear the mom shift gears, getting off her cajoling soapbox and leaning closer to her kid.

"Yes, honey, you did fall."

Tears began to stream down the child's face. "I fell because you made me ride around those corners. And I bumped that rock." Basically, it was Mom's fault.

"Well, honey, tell me what happened next?"

Pause. "I hurt myself. I scraped my knees."

"You did. Then what happened?"

Another pause. "Then I cried." As the playground fact checker, I could confirm this play-by-play. Not exactly edge-of-your-seat dialogue, but stick with me.

"And after you cried?"

Daughter paused. "Then I got back on my bike." She did. "And I was riding."

"And were you OK?" Mom asked.

"Yup, I was OK. I did three more loops." This is where we give the standing ovation for a beautiful parenting moment.

What was going on here? A few things. Mom was helping her child tell the story of what happened—revealing the implicit memory and making it explicit. While the implicit memory stores our experiences in the unconscious, explicit memory involves conscious reflection. Articulating the feeling of, "Oh my gosh, it was so scary. I fell!" brought this child's experience to the conscious level. Without this step, the memory will lurk within her mind and likely pop up in future fear and anxiety. She may not know the source of these feelings, but without processing the experience, she will hold on to that scary feeling of falling. The mom was not only giving her daughter the chance to recount what happened, she was helping her child complete the narrative; shaping the way her daughter related to the fall. Included in the story was the part where somehow, scrapes and all, *she got up*.

You may not be into bike riding (or playground observation), but we're all in the business of falling down. We tell ourselves stories about our soul scrapes, how hard it was, how scary it felt. We get so stuck on the negative that we forget to include the part where, despite the pain and difficulty, we did somehow find our way back up.

When that little girl wiped away her tears and remarked, "I was OK," she was practicing for redemption. How so? She was training herself to see that things can work out. Differently than expected? For sure. A few scars incurred? Absolutely. All part of rising up? One hundred percent. This mom was teaching her kid to own her narrative.

We can likewise shape our stories and become narrators in the moments when, with the help of the Almighty, we have gotten back to upright. Training for redemption is recounting our lives and finding where G-d's plot twists were just what we needed, even if we didn't like them. It's the practice of reflecting on our day and seeing how things somehow worked out. These acts train us for redemption because they help us to see the Divine hand supporting us behind the scenes.

Searching for the ways in which light illuminates the darkness helps us live in the present moment with a bit more hope. So, to the mom in the playground: Thanks for helping me get back on my bike. I'll be a little less scared the next time I fall.

**"This too is for the good."**

*(Taanis 21a)*

You *really* know who you are when you play cards with a kid. You quickly see your true nature: How competitive are you? Can you learn a new game from someone a fraction your age? For me, the next moment is realizing I can't shuffle, and am at the mercy of:

- Option A: Throw the cards on the table and scramble them up.
- Option B: Marvel at the fine motor skills of a junior card shuffler.

The real moment of truth was when, between Crazy Eights, Go Fish, and Gin Rummy, I discovered myself trying to win. Hoping—wishing—that the next card I turned over would be "that card." When a twinge of guilt over a winning hand emerged, I reminded myself that no one likes a sore loser, so really it was a public service to win—thereby giving others the chance to cultivate their good-loser skills.

Right. So selfless. Until the next round, when it was *my* turn to work on sportsmanship, and my earlier statement, "If you had fun, then you won," came back to haunt me. Let's face it, getting it right, feeling like you've "got this one," and "luck is in your hand," feels a whole lot better than accepting the hand you've been dealt with a smile.

Card games may seem inconsequential, but they might just be a training ground for figuring out how to play the much more important game of life. Learning how to play a hand, enjoy the game, *and* feel like a winner regardless of the outcome, requires redefining what it means to be a winner. I'm not suggesting we step out of the land of goals and objectives. I love a good win at the game of life—even more than shouting, "Spit!" and proclaiming myself a card champion—but do we sometimes become hyper-focused on the goal? It takes skill to care both about where we are going and how we get there.

Living in a world where we say, "I'm just playing for fun" makes it easy—because we let go of any investment in the outcome. On the other hand, only putting stock in the final result can leave us pouting, frustrated, and frankly, feeling like we've lost. This deflated feeling comes from devaluing the process and overinvesting in the external successes; we are paralyzed by disappointment when certain goals end up unattainable. The real art of card playing *and* life is knowing it's really about both the game and the goal.

Yes, playing cards reminded me of my competitive nature. It also pushed me to recall that no matter what the outcome—who won and what cards I was dealt—I could accept the process. It may be easier to take this perspective when all that's at stake is the king of hearts and a drop of ego.

But what about our challenging relationships? Or the losses we endure: death, finances, health, and security? Can we see them as equally useful parts of the journey?

The trick, just as card playing would show us, is not thinking we've won in the moment (because let's face it, often we don't), but embracing and trusting that there is meaning to the process itself. This shift requires us to stop fighting our challenges and start looking for the opportunities they bring. If we can do this, we truly win in life.

When all we want is the prize at the end—the job, the marriage, the baby, or the big break —it's hard to revel in the getting there. But it's the very work we do, the way we engage with the journey, that produces pleasure in the results. If all we want is to arrive, we will miss the beauty along the way. Like any good card player, we ought to pay attention to each hand, investing in the details of our days and considering our next move.

Goodness doesn't arrive in perfectly packaged parcels on our doorsteps. It sneaks in when we least expect—disguised sometimes in a losing hand. But if we are willing to dig deep, to lay down the need to look like we are winning, we will discover true triumph.

We may still like to win at cards, but we all have the power to transform our lives.

*"If you're never able to tolerate a little bit of pain and discomfort, you'll never get better."*

*(Angela Duckworth)*[3]

---

3    *Grit: The Power of Passion and Perseverance* (Toronto: Collins, 2016).

I have a love-hate relationship with homework.

I say this with respect for all you educators who swear by the work you send home. I'm simply speaking from my own experience. As a student, I didn't need cajoling to do my homework. It was just a fact of life—I did it. As a parent, I have more intense feelings.

Maybe it's easier to explain by relating the afterschool play-by-play: I pick up my daughter from school, check how her day was, deliver a snack, and ask: "What's the homework situation?" Typically, the answer is, "Not much." This can mean anything from twenty minutes to two hours. Then there is the golden answer: "I don't have any homework." Now, as a parent I get giddy—probably more excited than my child. The vistas of time between getting home and supper-bath-bed feel unending. The hobbies we can start...the trips to the park...the time for reading and chatting and...and...and...

So, all that to show you my aversion to the homework list she brings home.

Now let me tell you the other side of the story. I have also come to respect homework, perhaps *because* of my very resistance.

The goodness lurking in math problems, review, and reading comprehension, after a long day at school, is the difficulty itself. That is where I see some value in homework: cultivating the ability to do hard things, training us to value perseverance and patience in the face of *I don't feel like it*. I'll be honest—I need it as much as my daughter. I also struggle when it comes to tasks I'm afraid of, people I'd rather avoid, or work that feels overwhelming. When our inner voice asks, *When will this get easier?* and, *Why is this so hard?* it's a sign we have some spiritual homework of our own. It's not that we need times table review, but we can all benefit from leaning into the discomfort. I'm not suggesting we don't have our fair share of struggles, or even that we back down from challenges, but maybe how we look at them can use a little tweaking. If the value of homework is not only in the content, but in the skill of doing the hard work despite our resistance, then life might have some similar ways of stretching us. Just when we tell ourselves, *I'm done for the day*, the Almighty sends someone to test our patience. Where we are scared to speak up, we find ourselves needing to find our voice. We may want to run away, but the challenge will find us. *That* is the way of G-d-sent homework. Our job is to keep showing up.

We won't always get it right. We can't. Let's be honest—any kid with perfect work is going to make a teacher suspicious. But the kid who dutifully tries, who sits herself down and says, "I'm going to do my best," is truly the star student. The surefire sign that something is our homework is this: it's hard. It will come in the form of our kids, our bills, our parents, and our partners. It will creep up at the exact hour we feel we are done for the day/month/year. And then we get to decide: Will we say, "OK, Hashem, teach me. I'm here to learn," or are we going to side with the voice that says there's any easier way out?

The good part about homework is that it comes again and again. So even if we procrastinate or tantrum a bit, even if we try to wish it away, there will be another opportunity. It takes courage to endure. It requires strength to keep working away at life. We aren't born homework-ready. We build our grit each time we show up in the fear and discomfort. We become people who persist when we stay committed despite setbacks. The change comes through the doing; the doing comes to change us.

Next time we're sent a load of Heavenly homework, maybe we'll see it a little differently: with less resistance and more willingness. As for my daughter, I still celebrate the days when she answers, "I don't have any homework."

It started early in the week—the planning for the cold, cold weekend ahead. It had been a mild winter, but temperatures were set to plummet. The weather networks were reporting as if snow and cold had never before hit Canada. Given the ramped-up style of news reporting—weather included—one always has to take such predictions with a grain of salt; they often predict that snow will halt all traffic, and only a few flakes end up falling.

Still, for the cold-weather weary among us, warnings of -31 degrees Celsius is no laughing matter, particularly since I had plans that involved a late-evening Shabbos walk home. Advice started coming in early. "You'll need to layer," and, "Are you sure you want to go out?" were among the queries of my midweek correspondences. I was determined to stay the course. I was not going to be a weather wimp. I reassured all parties (perhaps most importantly, myself) that I would dress for the elements. I was reminded of a winter athlete's remark, "There is no such thing as bad weather...only poor preparation." I would be undeterred.

Sort of.

All was going as planned. Temperatures were dropping, Shabbos dinner plans were in place —thermal leggings, balaclava, and heavy-duty mittens had been purchased. Like a soldier for cold weather combat, I was armed and ready. And then, I found myself in front of a twenty-four-hour news feed, with the weather forecast displayed in the top right-hand corner of the screen. Visuals of clouds, sunshine, and snowflakes rolled over the weekend forecast, as did the sub-zero temperatures. Then there was the red tracking tape along the bottom of the screen, "Cold weather alert: extreme weather conditions." The first time I saw it, I barely read the words. The second time, it registered. By its tenth screen loop, I was feeling a little anxious. It wasn't long before I was reconsidering the whole plan.

What had I been thinking? Who did I really think I was? Prepared? Bundled? Could anything really protect me from the cold, the wind, and the finger stinging temperatures? My mind was racing, but I was determined not to be derailed.

In the end, I stayed the course. My Shabbos dinner hosts were well entertained by my winter wardrobe. With my full face mask, I looked more like a bank robber than a Canadian winter warrior. But when all was said and done, I got home safe, sound, and pretty warm.

So why all the drama throughout the week? What had happened to make me doubt my decision?

I'm talking about that moment when, watching the repeated warnings, the weather forecast over and over, uncertainty took hold. Something about the constant exposure, the messages shouting "It's gonna be hard! Stay on high alert!" sent me into a tailspin of self-doubt.

If cold weather warnings get our blood pressure up, what other messages taunt us daily? What makes us question our capacity to cope?

Surrounded by images and voices that tell us we might not have what it takes, be it beauty, money, or inner strength, we doubt our own abilities. We absorb these messages, translating them into our own inner voice and version of, "You're not good enough, you don't have what it takes." Once we hook into this thinking loop, much like that weather tracker, it's hard to get unstuck. These anxious thoughts are sometimes so automatic that we aren't aware of their presence. They become the background noise of our mind. Our work is to bring our thoughts into our conscious awareness. By becoming aware of our thinking, we create a space between our thoughts and ourselves. In that space we can observe thoughts for what they are: mental events that come and go just like the weather. Our choice lies in where we focus and what we hold on to.

We aren't going to eradicate scary weather forecasts any more than we will completely end anxious thoughts. They'll come and they'll go. Which means our power is in how we face our fear and doubt. It's always easier to make it through a storm—both outside and in our minds—when we are prepared. Which means we need to stock up on warm gear and inner strength. I managed to muster my courage only because I had been ready long before the forecasts flashed across the screen.

In much the same way, we can plan, bundling for the road ahead by getting clear about who we are. This means connecting to our inner worth, exploring what it means to be a soul, and building our relationship with G-d. These serve as buffers when the gale-force winds of self-doubt and fear pop up. The greater our internal clarity, the more we can stay steady when we come up against obstacles.

It's not about avoiding the elements; it's about preparing for them. Making time at the start of our day to check in with ourselves and with G-d can fundamentally shift how we experience the world. Developing practices that are grounding and remind us of our soul purpose shifts how we experience even the most challenging of days. Maybe you pause and breathe before entering your home, pray on your way to work, or take time to reflect at the day's end; finding your unique way to prepare is the key to making it through the storm of life. These daily practices can be anchors in times of stress. Challenges are non-negotiable; our control lies in how we ready ourselves.

Next time there's a cold weather snap, you might wish to stay in—but we can all use a little preparation when it comes to our thought storms.

*"When it feels that the earth that supported you has been irreparably overturned, there is a promise that new seedlings will one day take root and grow."*

*(Sherri Mandell)*[4]

We were mid-supper when we first heard the sirens. We took note and returned to eating. Then there was a second set of sirens. And a third. And a faint billow of smoke visible from the window. And so, supper interruptions began. Hovering near the window we ascertained a fire only a few houses down the block. Red engines, ambulances, and cop cars began to fill the street.

I have to qualify this by sharing my slight fascination with emergency services and first responders. I am in awe. I am curious. So, it wasn't long before supper was left to grow cold and we were traipsing along the street to see what was happening.

There is a fine line between interest and nosiness. I would never advocate rubbernecking where our gaze does not belong. After stopping to pray for everyone's safety and pausing to contemplate next steps, it seemed pretty clear: we needed to check this out.

From my narrow vantage point, I could make out a ladder extended from the fire truck to the rooftop. The fire hose had been hooked up to nearby hydrants and there was a steady stream of firefighters in and out of the house. My heart broke, watching this family home destroyed. I imagined the memories made in kitchen corners engulfed in flames. A lifetime of building, instantly gone.

Yet, I was also mesmerized by the scene: How often in a lifetime would we merit to observe firsthand the courage, know-how, and grit it takes

---

4    *The Road to Resilience: From Chaos to Celebration* (New Milford: Toby Press, 2015).

to fight a fire? What a blessing to live in a country where people are willing and able to fight to keep us safe, where we have an infrastructure in place to support these shining red trucks and whirring sirens. Can one be a stone's throw from such an event and not pause to wonder at the unfolding before our eyes? So, there we were, making our way to the crowd of "concerned neighbors" watching the real-life-drama unfold.

It soon became clear that no one had been hurt. Thank G-d. Even without injuries, putting out a fire was no small feat. As firefighters emerged covered in soot, another began to climb across the ladder, propped up on the roof, with a chainsaw in hand. We watched as he cut open a square shaped hole in the roof, and with the help of another firefighter, inserted a hose down into the attic.

I will not give you the entire play-by-play. Suffice to say that we had to pull ourselves away much sooner than the curtain fell on the scene. Hours into the evening they were still hard at work and I was still mulling over the G-d-size message to be decoded. Over the following days we checked in on the house. A dumpster out front. A news report of the fire. Workers in and out the side door. Firetruck excitement had left, but act two was just beginning. Destruction might come in a day, but sifting through the rubble and rebuilding is a slower process.

As much as the fire—its fighters and the extraordinary neighborhood scene—was a sight to behold, it has been the aftermath that is most instructive. While signs and wonders come to get our attention, it's what we do in their wake that defines us. It is in our most vulnerable times, when the framework of our life is stripped away, that we are forced to dig deep within.

Staring destruction in the face—be it a house fire, the end of a relationship, or a life goal not met—we can choose to search out growth and hope. It's in the moments when we feel broken down that we are sent a chance to rebuild. Some days, it's a moment-by-moment choice to look for G-d's kindnesses in our lives. It's often disguised as the stretching of a fire ladder, a neighbor's smile, or even a bumper sticker that makes us laugh. There are moments when our job is to simply show up and watch with awe, seeing clearly the signs sent our way.

And then we must take all that we have witnessed and ask: What am I going to build now? If we can muster the courage to keep moving forward, we have accepted our mission. We are wired to grow through adversity. The ability to overcome challenges is not something we can build in the absence of challenges. Crisis and hardship are where we cultivate resilience, which means every bump along the way is really an opportunity to discover our inner resources, our next move, and our capacity to rise. We don't need to wait for a fire or fiasco to build this mentality. Everyday glitches are tests that serve as a practice ground: we can look for the good, the ways we can learn and grow, wherever we are.

I remain grateful to those firefighters and in awe of all the ways Hashem sends help and messengers along the way.

*"Hope to Hashem, strengthen yourself and He will give you courage, and hope to Hashem."*

*(Tehillim 27:14)*

A friend and I were out for a leisurely stroll on a country road. I don't remember hearing it, but I do recall the sensation of pure terror running up my spine. I froze. We grabbed onto each other. Only then did I register the sound: a dog. I looked to my right to see a rottweiler dashing toward us up the lawn of a cottage. This was no puppy; more like the winner of the "canines that nightmares are made of" contest. We let out a scream. The dog froze at the property edge. It continued to bark but remained a few feet away. I could feel my heart racing, like it was trying to break free from my body.

Clutching hands, we picked up our pace. Still shaking, we recounted the incident. "I didn't even know where the sound was coming from. I panicked." It didn't matter that the dog was likely harmless. The startling situation had sent us straight into fight-or-flight mode, and we were left to deal with its aftermath.

A threat—real or imagined—has us running for cover or readying for a dual. This is how we are wired to survive. But what about the times when the danger isn't real; rather, it's something we *perceive* as scary, like public speaking or filing taxes—decidedly difficult, but not actually dangerous. And so, comes part two of our dog story...

We continued along the road as the adrenaline slowly drained from our systems. Then came our predicament: getting back. The only way to return was the way we came. Which meant one thing. We would need to pass by the loud and protective rottweiler, thus revisiting our fear.

The fun thing about nervous systems is that they are quick learners. It doesn't take long to train yourself to fear a bear or avoid oncoming traffic. It's the wisdom of the body's protection system. So, you can understand why we felt nervous about walking back the way we came.

I guess there was another option: never go back. We could keep walking and literally never go back. We'd find new homes and jobs, abandoning our lives because we just couldn't go back. In some ways, this was appealing. Why bother retracing our steps when we could eternally evade that dog?

As absurd as it sounds, it's an option most of us have tried in one form or another—going to great efforts to avoid people, places, and memories that feel too painful or scary. In this case, there was only one way: forward. We couldn't perpetually avoid. We would have to forge ahead and face our fear.

Going back meant bracing for another meeting with the dog. Each cottage we passed brought us one step closer to that barking menace, but as we drew nearer, hearts racing, we also built a little courage and the sense that we could make it past. And we did. He barked, we walked, and it was over, a drop less scary than the first time.

You may not pass a rottweiler any time soon, but you will be faced with daily choices: to approach or avoid. When things don't go well on the first (or fiftieth) round, we may think it's time to throw in the towel. When we pray and the answers we want don't come, or we work and the project meets roadblocks, we may conclude it's time to give up. Tired of circling back, we avoid stressful situations, family conflicts, or that pile of bills; as if staying away will resolve the issue or make it disappear. In the moment, it's appealing, a temporary reprieve from the challenge—but avoidance keeps us stuck, living in fear and unable to move on.

If there's rottweiler wisdom for us, it's that our soul work is not a one-time event. It's an ongoing mission of repeatedly approaching, trying, and hoping. As scary as that dog's bark was, it can be even more terrifying to hope in the face of frustration, to love in an uncertain world. That is our mission—to find a way forward. To courageously hold onto faith, even when it's scary, to keep praying despite disappointment. As for the rottweiler, I'll still keep my distance.

## YOUR TURN: GUIDE QUESTIONS

- What is one mistake you have learned from in your life? How can you learn from a current hardship?
- Who role-models resilience for you? What is it about them that enables them to be resilient? How would you like to emulate them?
- What is something that you are avoiding because you are afraid of failing? Is there one small thing you can do to face that fear?
- What is changing in your life right now? How can you embrace that change and find new possibilities?

# CHAPTER 3

# Growth

"Rabbi Shimon said: Every single blade of grass has a corresponding angel in the sky that hits it and tells it to grow."

*(Midrash Rabbah, Bereishis* 10:6)

*"Hashem is close to the brokenhearted."*

*(Tehillim 34:19)*

It's the great controversy of spring. The dandelion debate: flower or weed? The conversation in my car went something like this:

"Mommy, look at all the dandelions."

Me, kicking into high-gear-mom-talk-mode: "Yes honey, aren't they beautiful? Isn't it funny, they look like flowers even though they are weeds."

Long pause from the back seat. "What do you mean they are weeds?" Fair question.

In trying to answer, I had to call deep upon my horticultural courage…and realize that I really know very little, if anything, about the classification of weeds, flowers, or how wildlife behaves. I stopped and started a couple of times. I restated the facts: dandelions equal weeds, not flowers. This educational technique (not too surprisingly) seemed to fall short of brilliant.

"Mommy," she replied, "they're not weeds. They're dandelions." No debating. No reclassifying. No ambivalence as to its flower-versus-weed status. Reality rolled out just as it was: plain and simple.

Sometimes a dandelion is just that: a dandelion. With all our efforts at fancy footwork, describing and classifying...we circle back to simplicity. We may try to explain their surprising beauty, we may wish to communicate the challenges of unwanted growth...but sometimes those boxes of reality are too confining.

- A weed suggests something that needs to be removed. Something unwanted. Something that requires fixing.
- A flower, on the other hand, tends to evoke visions of beauty, growth, and pleasure.

What we need at times is an in-between category—a way to accept something, or someone, *as is*. Somewhere between weed and flower is the dandelion reality of our lives: the person that calls for us to step down from our fix-it soapbox and love them...as they are. Before they can improve, we need to accept them in their current state.

We all need to be seen and valued for who we are. It's from this experience that we find the capacity to expand. The irony of always trying to change someone is that it holds them back. Think about the difference between someone telling you, "You're not good enough, so please change, and then I'll accept you" versus "I love you. I'm with you. How can we make this better?" The first approach shuts us down, the second primes us for growth. If we feel safe and understood, we are more willing to take risks and make changes. When we are caught up with, "How am I going to fix this?" "Is this a weed or a flower?" "A keeper or a loser?" there isn't much space to notice the beauty and love-worthiness before our eyes.

We live in a fractured world filled with pain and disconnection. Our mission is the soul-work of healing and repair. Just like the baby who first needs love and calming before she can grow and learn, so too our loved ones beg for our presence. We are called to stop thinking and analyzing and first love another for their dandelion-beauty: an admixture of flower beauty and weed-like faults. Loving in this way brings a deeper closeness and creates the possibility for growth at its own pace and in its own way.

It is no wonder that the dandelion grows so enthusiastically. She covers so much ground. She is fearless. She can be both the broken and the beautiful at once. In the brokenhearted moments of our days, the "weed times" of life, we too can grow like the dandelion. It is our imperfect relationships that teach us about accepting our own humanity. It is not from the fix-it-and-forget-it parts of our story that we learn to love deeply. When we embrace both the flaws and the beauty, we discover that some things in life are both flower and weed. If we can love each other with that awareness, we will inch closer to our soul purpose. As for the spring time, let's step out of the dandelion debate and start loving them as they are.

I was driving on the wrong side of the road. The workman was waving his arms, but I couldn't make sense of which way he wanted me to go. I had to circle back. Once again, he started waving me to the other side. I rolled down my window to ask him where exactly I ought to go.

"Ma'am, you're driving on the wrong side. There's wet paint here!" He hollered at me with aggravation. I felt a knot in my stomach.

Roadwork can bring out the upset in most of us.

"I'm sorry you're having a hard day, but please don't yell at me," I replied. Without missing a beat, he retorted, "I'm not having a hard day, you're just driving on the wrong side." Fair enough. "Well *I'm* having a hard day, so please don't yell at me!" I responded, tears welling up.

I must have caught him off guard. Here he was trying to direct traffic and paint the roadway, and now he had a crying woman on his hands. I was also surprised: I didn't realize I was that upset (or having a hard day) until I blurted it out.

"I'm sorry you're having a hard day, ma'am. I hope it gets better." I thanked him and drove off, still shaken by the encounter.

As I collected myself, I reflected on our conversation. Yes, it had felt uncomfortable to be in the wrong and confused about the directions, but there was another lesson here: what I had said to the workman was more about me and my experience. *I* was having a hard day. *I* didn't want to be yelled at. It would have been easy to dismiss it as an annoying interaction or blame him. Of course, hollering in aggravation *isn't* the right thing to do, but my words also reflected something about me, what had been going on in *my* life and how *I* was feeling.

It's easy to contemplate my reaction when I'll never see that workman again, and little hinges on our connection. It's more challenging to look at our emotions and responses in closer relationships. When we see a fault in someone else, feel jealous or upset with their behavior, it's a chance to ask, "What is this telling me about *myself*?" What bothers us is a compass pointing inward, revealing our personal soul work.

I was upset by how the workman had yelled. Fair enough. But he also held up a mirror when he replied, "I'm sorry *you're* having a hard day"; it made it clear that this was also about me. If we want to live in a better world, if we crave deeper connection and peaceful relationships—we need to *be* that change. There's a tendency to place all the blame on others and turn away from uncomfortable feelings. When we do that, we miss an opportunity.

If instead we turn toward these thoughts and experiences, they can become our personal guides. Like markers pointing the way to our inner work, our reactions carry deep wisdom. The friend who makes us jealous is a chance to look at our own lives. The person who irritates or annoys is showing us our own impatience. An unkind encounter is an opening for self-compassion. We can run away, or we can accept the invitation to look into that mirror and see who we can become and the world we can create.

I'm sure there are people who would have yelled back at that workman. I made a different choice that day. And with my words, we both softened, becoming less defensive and more connected. Who knows how his day was changed. Was he nicer to the next driver? Did he smile a bit more? If nothing else, *he and I* shared a moment of kindness.

How we live, including our on-the-road-workman conversations, will be the world we inhabit. When we build ourselves and open our hearts, we will find that energy reflected back. I drove on that same road yesterday. The paint job is completed, and the workman is gone; but I was reminded of our encounter and the opening it created.

*"This world is like a lobby before the World to Come; prepare yourself in the lobby so that you may enter the banquet hall."*

(Pirkei Avos 4:16)

I love almost everything about hotels: mini shampoos, ice machines, and the feeling when you first walk into your room and check out the bed and the amenities of your temporary home.

Even if I haven't traveled far.

Even if it's not a fancy hotel.

As long as the key to the room works and it's clean, the little girl inside of me comes out to play. She feels like real life is suspended. Responsibilities and daily stresses are put on hold, replaced by smiling staff and promises of housekeeping service in the morning.

Now that I have proclaimed my love of hotels, let me also tell you why I *adore* hotel lobbies—it's where the magic begins. It's where I first survey the scene, take in the fancy hotel scent, and am welcomed to my temporary abode.

When I arrive at a hotel lobby, I have a Pavlovian response. I start to feel excited, certain there's something good waiting on the other side. And that is the truth—the lobby, in all its splendor, is hinting at something more intimate, personal, and uniquely enriching.

No one wants to live in the lobby. We know that it is a place of arrival, yet at the same time it is transitory—that is what makes it so alluring. "Come! Stay here!" The lobby holds promises of relaxation, pampering, and rejuvenation. Yet we don't get confused and think the lobby of the Hilton or the Marriot is meant to be a place of permanence.

When it comes to our lives, however, we mistakenly think it's about arriving—that a career, a relationship, or simple comfort and security mean we have permanently landed. That is not the final destination, it was never meant to be.

This world is the training ground of the soul. Every person, place, and challenge is designed to build us and is individually prescribed for our personal growth. Just as we visit hotels, our soul is likewise on a transitory journey. This world is not the final destination.

When we understand that the details of life are elements in a soul curriculum and that we are only passing through, it changes how we relate to the everyday. The annoying coworker becomes a practice ground for patience, the heartbreaking loss is transformed into an opportunity for deeper healing. With this perspective, nothing is without meaning and everything is designed to teach us.

Immense enjoyment of hotels is fine. Getting excited to take the elevator up and discover the layout of the room is lovely. But getting confused and thinking that the final goal is in this world means we have missed the point. When we come to see our lives as the lobby, we can take pleasure in this world, knowing that it is merely a gateway.

With this awareness, we can leverage every experience as a means to build our soul-selves. When we realize we've decided to camp out in a hotel lobby, we have unlocked the secret to a whole new way of being. Each joy and challenge becomes a training ground, and we know that the pleasures of hotels, lobbies, and lovely adventures are but a hint to the World to Come.

Sunday Night Syndrome. That feeling of dread before the back-to-reality work or school week begins. The heaviness in my limbs that calls out, "No! Just one more day," as if pushing off tomorrow will somehow make it easier.

We make our way toward Monday morning like a roller coaster fueled by angst. Part of the ride usually involves chugging up the roller coaster ramp, the telltale slow down as it ascends and the feeling of the gears going, "*ch-chug, ch-chug,*" as we near the peak. Our mind calls out with anxiety, "Abort! Abort!" because we believe that we can't handle what's coming next. Sometimes it's Monday morning we fear, other times it's our job, a relationship, or another life challenge. When we think it's more than we can manage, we are in the grips of Sunday Night Syndrome.

Showing up for Monday mornings can happen in any hour or day. These are the moments when, fully strapped into the roller coaster of our lives, we feel ourselves careening forward—and rather than fighting the forward momentum, we allow the movement itself to carry us. Instead of running from the demands and the people in our life, we step up and accept each challenge as it comes.

Acceptance is not a passive act. In fact, it usually takes a whole lot of work to stop resisting our reality. It requires looking at the challenges before us and instead of avoiding them, facing them head-on. This means keeping that appointment that makes us anxious, having the difficult conversation with our kid, or showing up to another lonely afternoon and trusting that this is exactly where we need to be. Acceptance means letting go of the belief that life would be better if only we were smarter, thinner, had a different husband or job, a nicer house, or fewer stresses. Experience has likely shown you that efforts to dream your way to a different reality are futile, wasted energy. We may try to wish away our circumstances or fixate on all that is "wrong," but we discover time and again that this doesn't solve the problem. How would life be different if we could loosen our grip, release a little bit of fear, and trust that we *do* have what it takes to manage? Can we see that all the pieces of our lives are exactly what our soul needs to fulfill its mission?

When we are stuck in fear, there is little room for hope or possibility. In those times, it's hard to believe that we *can* manage. So we fight our reality, criticizing others, ourselves, or avoid the issues altogether. The problem is, the more we protest, the less capable we are of managing change. We can't make changes if we're not willing to first be with things as they are. This is the magic of acceptance: only by way of accepting our reality will it begin to shift.

I'm not suggesting that we fall in love with Monday mornings, stressful days, or difficult nights. I am saying that when we relax into the experience and accept life on G-d's terms, we find a greater ability to cope, new reserves of strength, and untapped possibilities. When we stop dreading and start living, we may just discover a new way of being. Holding on tight to, "I don't want to be here!" is the way toward feeling stuck. Letting go, even as that roller coaster plummets, is the route to acceptance.

We may still get anxious Sunday night. We don't need to be fans of that Monday morning feeling. But we can also work on being with life as it is, because Monday mornings come every week. We can put our energy into building today instead of trying to fight off tomorrow.

*"How shall we sing Hashem's song in a foreign land?"*

(*Tehillim 137:4*)

There are certain dreams I can depend on having when I'm feeling worried about being unprepared or overwhelmed. They usually involve an upcoming French or math test for which I haven't studied.

Pretty classic—those were my worst subjects in school.

In my dream, it's the day of the test, and I haven't even cracked the book. Or I am staring down at dancing numbers and have no clue what to do. It doesn't matter that I dropped French over twenty years ago, or that I seem to be getting by well enough with my basic arithmetic skills. When I feel unprepared, worry floods me like I'm back in school and haven't studied.

I have a similar dream, but this one is about packing. I still vividly remember a nightmare I had the summer before I went away to overnight camp for the first time. The bus was pulling up to our house, and then it was pulling away without me, all as I leaned over my half-packed duffel bag. Eek!

Pretty transparent worries. Equally universal. What's the concern? What is the gut-gnawing feeling we all recognize in those dreams? That we don't have what it takes to get "there," wherever our "there" is: passing the test, getting on the bus to camp, making the flight. When we believe that we don't have enough, we feel stuck and frightened. In this state, we see no way out.

What is the message hidden in our fear? There's some wisdom calling to us from the dreamworld. Realizing that we aren't yet "there," that we are living in an incomplete and not-yet-ready state, is an uncomfortable wake-up call. We are in exile, living in a world that is disconnected from G-d and largely devoid of spirituality. When we open our eyes to this reality, we have a choice to make: go back to sleep and try to numb out the pain of exile, or have the courage to stay awake, with all the pain and responsibility that brings. It's not easy to hope for a better world or champion spirituality and meaning. But the alternative of remaining in the nightmare of exile is even scarier.

Flights can be rebooked, tests retaken, and subjects dropped. But when it comes to our lives, we cannot afford to go back to sleep. We need only read headlines or talk to our friends to realize the suffering around us. We are steeped in exile. Anxiety dreams might seem trivial, but the sense that we need to get on our A game, try harder, and be kinder, is not an illusion. If there is one thing my dreams are teaching me today, it's that in the land of staying awake we can point ourselves toward redemption—toward a world where we clearly feel G-d's presence and live our soul purpose.

About a year ago, my friend announced she'd be moving her business. So, after a grueling year of renovations, a temporary location, the ending of a partnership, and building permit roadblocks, this friend finally opened her new location.

This didn't mean the renovations were finished. It was more of a "'soft opening," including workers applying caulk and installing exposed plumbing. But she was under pressure: multiple delays and a slew of unforeseen challenges meant there was no more wiggle room. If you've worked with a contractor or even set a time line for leaving the house with a toddler, you know that sometimes we just get out when we can, mess and all. As a card-carrying citizen of the world of imperfection, I wasn't fazed by the still-rustic look of the place.

Later that day I sent my friend a message: *Just wanted to say I was in the new space—it was great! Mazel tov! I am inspired by your vision, persistence, and courage*. No reply. No worries. I wasn't expecting one. I just wanted to send a virtual pat on the back. It seemed like she might need one.

Clearly G-d wanted us to speak because I "bumped into her" later that day.

"Thanks for your message!" She smiled.

"I just wanted to let you know it looks great," I assured her. "I know it's been quite a process."

Her smile softened as she quipped, "Oh yes. And it's not over yet..."

I could see that. And therein lies the beauty. The unfinished business of reality was laid out for all to see. There was no pretending that this project had gone as planned. None of us were under the impression that life, or this business, was tied up with a neat little bow. And for that I wanted to hug her. To say thank you. Because I'm also under renovation. I am also dealing with unexpected challenges and stumble on parts of myself gripped by fear and uncertainty. Like mid-renovation exposed wiring, these feelings are part of a life in process. It's a relief when we acknowledge that we are all living in this state of imperfection.

Normalizing and validating our struggle is not enough. It is the beginning. When we see the brokenness in ourselves, when we glimpse a fracture in our world—we have a choice to make: turn away in fear or find the courage to keep showing up.

I am grateful that my friend opened her business doors before everything was perfect. It gave us all permission to be more honest about our imperfections. The light fixtures are being installed and the paint will dry, but I will always see the layer underneath, *because I was there for the process*. I know that, much like myself, behind the paint and nice finishes is a deeper story of struggle. And *that* is where our greatness lies: in facing the unfinished parts of ourselves and choosing to keep working and growing.

Perhaps next time you walk by a renovation you'll look at it with different eyes. You'll see it as the Almighty's reminder that we are all merely works in progress. Maybe it will even give you a bit of courage to keep showing up. I know it helps me. So, I'll see you out there among the "wet paint" signs.

*"A person's imagination has no limits."*

*(Rabbi Yisrael Salanter)*

Around her tenth birthday, my daughter came home from gymnastics describing the technique required for a "throwback." I admit I am still unclear about the specifics of the move, but I learned a lot about the required technique.

Standing with her feet hip-distance apart, she carefully explained.

"Imagine you are holding a ball. Then try to kick it up in the air and flip back like you're watching it." Never one for ball sports, it seems my athleticism is limited even when it's make-believe. But there my daughter stood, picturing that object in its fullness—and, through the seeing itself, her movements launched.

Teachers and coaches often use strategies of imagery. I recall my ballet instructor telling us to imagine a string pulling up at the top of our heads to help us stand straight. Competitive athletes are told to envision their winning moments, crossing the finish line, achieving their personal best. Theory goes that if the mind's eye can conjure it, the body will follow. The wisdom of junior gymnastics instruction seemed to be about far more than a throwback. I could see the ball because she could see it. She imagined it as if it were real.

In a world where seeing is believing, we may sometimes feel like we are walking around holding imaginary balls. We believe in something—goodness, growth, connection, G-d—but the world, with all its darkness and doubt, has us questioning the substance of what we carry. Other times our eyes can't seem to conjure an image at all. Scrounging for hope or direction, we seem to find nothing in our sight line. Then, because we can't picture it, we think it simply doesn't exist. Our eyes tell us this is all there is, and we buy in, thinking that if we haven't found that thing (be it a ball to kick back, a hand to hold, or a hint of light) we never will. But as that gymnastics coach knew, just because something isn't visible to the naked eye, it doesn't mean it can't or doesn't already exist.

If our greatest challenges were mastering gymnastics moves, we might all become expert "imaginers." We'd spend hours visualizing those balls, kicks, and tumbles in the service of our success. When the feat is more than a cartwheel, the same strategy can be just as powerful. When we want to act in a certain way, when we want to live in a world where we choose patience over anger, trust over fear, and light over darkness, we can actually practice and create those realities in our imagination.

This exercise might mean sitting in our driveway before entering the house and picturing ourselves calmly dealing with cranky kids, or perhaps visualizing ourselves making it through a tough conversation without falling apart. In much the same way that the body follows the imagined string pulling us straight, it will likewise follow the mind that dreams of growth, grace under fire, and the ability to feel connected in our most challenging times.

Picturing a ball between our hands might be the best place to start. In the moment that I saw the imaginary object, I realized that the eyes don't see it all. There are moments when the not-yet-here reality can indeed be imagined. This strategy is powerful because it can change our self-concept. When we see ourselves as the kind of people who behave like our better selves, we can make that self a reality. If I picture myself as a woman who gets back up regardless, or if my daughter sees herself as a hard worker, we will rise to those standards.

I will never be able to do a throwback. There are likewise unrealized dreams in my life, but I'm picturing who I can be and what I might become. When we do this, no matter where or what the challenge, we are able to take one more step forward—for we have imagined ourselves as that kind of person.

*"It's a tree of life to all those who take hold of it, those who hold fast will be blessed."*

*(Mishlei 3:18)*

I was trying to balance in tree pose.

For the yoga-uninitiated, this involves standing on one foot. The teacher had instructed us to focus on one unmoving spot to help find some stability as we endeavored to balance. Standing in the part of the studio where shoes are stored, I focused on a pair on a shelf a couple inches higher than the top of my head.

I reached that place of stillness.

For a moment. And then I began to wobble.

Teeter-totter. I fell right out of the pose.

"Falling is part of the practice," the instructor reminded us. I resumed the pose, and this time, I wondered if I might find a spot at eye level, maybe that would hold me more at center. And so, I set my sights upon the shelf right at eye level. There sat two pairs of shoes, one balanced upon the other. Fixing my gaze, I found some steadiness in the pose. Deep breath in. Exhale. I felt supported and strong. Funny, I thought, that I had initially wanted to look up higher, when in truth, the spot right ahead was most conducive to balancing. And then I started to study those shoes. Their angle. The curve of the heel. The color. And the brand name: "Answer." From within the stillness of tree pose I let out an internal chuckle. The answer had been there all along: Look straight ahead. It's where to find our answers...

Walking through our lives searching can lead us in all sorts of directions. As people who seek growth, many of our pursuits bring us insight and clarity. Chasing dreams, digging deep within, and asking the hard questions of ourselves and the world is the work we are here to do. Wrestling with our experience of life and G-d's place in it is our soul mission, our job as spiritual beings in a physical world. Yet sometimes the search leads us astray. We may ask for advice, buy the latest self-help books, or sign up for the newest cure/program/cleanse, but are we searching too far afield? Do we crave clarity with such passion that we fail to stop long enough to notice "the answer," the direction or inner knowledge that is here, right before our eyes?

Understanding our purpose is an ongoing process. Like standing wobbly in the tree pose of life, we may fall, we may fix our sights too high, too low, or on a spot more appropriate for someone else. It's not about getting it right on the first go; it's about staying committed to the process, one where we ask questions and pay careful attention to the answers. It also means training our gaze closer to home. It's tempting to think that newer or different is better; that is what the world at large will tell us.

When we open ourselves to this experience we make space for G-d's wisdom. We come from a rich tradition, a long line of individuals who have wrestled with the Divine, mining the depths of Torah for answers. Wired into our spiritual DNA is the capacity to contend with the world and all its complexity, to find G-d within the struggle. Hidden within the Torah are the answers we most crave. Our work is to look deeply at the source so we can unearth its riches. We rob ourselves of this opportunity when we launch on a frantic search—running far and looking high and low—missing what's right before our eyes. It's not that we don't struggle, wobble, and fall; it's that we find balance again and again when we stay engaged in the process of learning and growing through G-d's guidebook for living.

I walked away from that yoga class with a smile on my face. I know what it's like to forget where to ask my questions and how to find the way. I also know what it's like to be reminded that the answers are here. My job? Our collective mission? To keep looking and asking. I'll see you out there.

There's a weekly feature in the paper that I love called, "Spot the Difference." I don't think I'm their target audience…it's in the children's section.

You're probably familiar with the format. Two pictures almost the same, side by side; the task is to find the minor differences between the two. At first glance, they seem identical. But once you start looking, you see that there really are slight variations. The first few items emerge easily enough. Then it gets harder. I begin to wonder if there is anything more to find. Herein lies the moment of truth. It's so tempting to give up. I have the same reaction to puzzles. I was once convinced that a nine-piece puzzle was actually missing a piece as I tried to coach my then four-year-old in the task. I was wrong. What I needed was a little more patience and spatial reasoning.

Glancing between the two Spot the Difference pictures, it comes down to one question: Will I stick with this long enough to notice the details, or will I abandon the challenge altogether? The following week, the paper publishes a list of the answers from the previous issue, titled, "Did You Spot the Differences?" The question is illuminating. Did I stick with the challenge long enough to find the details, or did I throw in the towel because I got tired, bored, or discouraged?

This is, in essence, the daily test of a busy life. Are we able to stay present, notice the details, and persevere when faced with difficulties? I am among the more impatient in the crowd; I want all the answers now. I'm pretty sure I'm in good company. We want all the results now (or even better, yesterday). But that's just not how the universe unfolds. Spiritual shifts and lasting change tend to come in subtle adjustments. That might just be the Heavenly message of "Spot the Difference."

Seeing the differences between yesterday and today may be imperceptible to the naked eye. But a well-trained soul knows we have to stay the course. Keep searching. Keep working. Over time we can be the people we dreamed of becoming. It is easy to get discouraged. We slip into fatigue and disappointment. But if we remain steadfast, we will see that we have changed. When we can react differently to a problem, there is a slight shift in our character. Little by little.

In the meantime, we are living in the potential. We are the works in progress of our future selves. Living this way requires trusting that there will be change if we continue to strive for growth. Just because we can't see Hashem's plan, or don't understand the timeline of our lives, doesn't mean it will always be this way. Clarity will come; we will look back at these days with knowing eyes, spotting all the ways today has become the tomorrow we needed. In the meantime, it takes trust in the process. If we give up now, who knows what greatness we will miss? Things are changing. We are changing. We just have to step back every once in a while and notice.

My daughter and I were on a day-long trail of errands, so bumping into an acquaintance while shopping was a little reprieve from our on-a-mission mentality. I hadn't seen her in a while and it was nice to catch up. She was bubbly and sweet, chatting with us as we made our way about the store. We kept up the conversation while I sorted through shirt sizes, and we lingered at the cash register before parting ways on to the next errand. As we left, there was something about her warmth that stuck with me. I didn't think much of it, but I must have carried that feeling of sweet connection out of the store, along with our purchases.

That night, I dreamed about her. In my dream, I bumped into her parents. I was excited to see them, relating that I had seen their daughter that day. In fact, it was such a pleasure—her smiling face and cheerful manner—that I reported, "She was so lovely, she was like a ray of sunshine in the middle of the store, she brightened our day!" Now, to be clear, she really was all of that, and while I like flowery language, that just isn't a phrase I've ever used. When I awoke, I couldn't help but smile, because there was someone I knew who *would* have said exactly that—my Bubby.

I couldn't help but feel like my Bubby had spoken those words. That was her way, to speak from the heart, to describe a personality with such passion, "Like a ray of sunshine." I could even hear her intonation. Yet, there *I* was, in my dreamworld, piling on praises, calling upon imagery, and feeling like they were my own words. It was as if a voice had emerged from within me, one that was both learned and my own. Part of my Bubby's gift was her ability to make everyone around her feel special. Her love and attention was a bit like fairy dust, leaving admirers in its wake. It seemed as though this quality that my Bubby possessed had been awakened inside of me.

While I had bumped into this young woman during the day, I had bumped into a dormant part of my soul during the night. Maybe my dream was hinting to something: those might have been my Bubby's words, but they belonged to my soul. In my nighttime expression, I had stumbled upon a deeper truth: that planted within my spiritual DNA is an even greater capacity for kindness and passionate expression.

We come with inborn potential, wired with soul genetics much like our physical cells. Our mission is to unearth these genes and give them expression in the world. When I bumped into that young woman, I'd had a chance to both experience and express a part of my soul-self.

We are each born with a G-dly spark planted within our soul, giving us a deep sense of purpose and connection. The world and its darkness makes us forget our holy mission. We confuse the bodily experience with our essence, thinking that we are the sum total of our jobs and accomplishments, our bodies and our bios. When physical experiences and résumé-worthy achievements become our measure of self-worth, we become estranged from our essence. Our mission is to awaken our soul-self, the part inside that knows who she is, where she comes from, how important her contributions are to the world, and how beloved she is to her Creator.

We all have this knowledge inside because we are all a drop of G-d. As humans, we live the ultimate paradox: the Infinite Source of all life residing within our finite and mortal bodies. We don't need to search far or scale mountains to find the Divine—it's right here inside of us.

I may have woken up from my dream, but spiritual awakening is an ongoing process. If we want to discover our personal mission, we need only look to our lives. Our strengths and interests, the people we meet and the wisdom we learn are the guideposts for our souls, showing us our unique purpose here on earth.

We don't need to recreate ourselves, but rather *rediscover* what's been waiting within all along. This is why when we learn a deep piece of wisdom, it feels less like a new discovery and more like recognizing an old friend. Why? Because it was ours all along—we just needed to re-find it.

I believe my dream was waking me up to the part of my soul that *is* like my Bubby and shares a piece of her wisdom. I'm hoping I can hold onto a little bit of that clarity, and who knows? Maybe I'll even describe someone as "a ray of sunshine."

## YOUR TURN: GUIDE QUESTIONS

- Is there a part of yourself or your life that you're afraid of accepting? Can you try telling yourself that you fully accept yourself and life as it is? What is it like when you stop fighting reality? Are you better able to cope? Try practicing this at regular intervals throughout your day. What do you notice?
- Who are the people in your life who need help? Where do you see brokenness in the world? What is one small way you can take responsibility today? Take action: call that friend, give that child a hug, or make a donation to a cause.
- Where do you want your life to change? Are you impatient or judgmental with yourself? How does that get in the way of your growth? Instead of focusing on your shortcomings, can you see the small ways that you are growing? Can you build an appreciation for incremental change?
- What are the unique circumstances and challenges of your life? How might the Almighty be asking you to grow? Where do you think your personal Divine curriculum is pointing you?

# CHAPTER 4
# Trust

"The one who trusts in Hashem, kindness
surrounds him…"
(*Tehillim* 32:10)

We stood waiting to cross the street, three women in a row. To my far right was a businesswoman in sunglasses with a focused look on her face. Wedged between us was a mom with a stroller, the hood pulled over her passenger, leaving only little legs and Crocs in view. Our silent waiting was interrupted by the tumble of a sippy cup.

Businesswoman and I both looked up and locked eyes. Time seemed to slow as we lunged in unison for the cup. Almost knocking heads, we exchanged a laugh and lifted the sacred sippy cup. Accepting the cup, the mom commented, "Thanks, she's just falling asleep, so she let go." We three shared a smile as we crossed the street.

Parting ways, the mom's words stayed with me: "She's just falling asleep, so she let go." What a contrast to me and businesswoman, who were on such high alert we nearly concussed in our efforts to help. I hadn't seen the child's face, but I imagined that sweet look of half-sleep overcoming her. I pictured a little hand slowly loosening its grip on the cup without a worry about where it would land. Of course not, Mom will get it. I marveled at how a sense of trust can transform something as simple as a hold on a cup and as great as a grip on reality.

Feeling safe and secure fundamentally shifts how we live. When we think that we will be OK, we are open and able to manage almost any challenge. If we trust that even if we fall or fail we can recover, then we are willing to take risks, try new things, and be vulnerable. Cultivating a sense of trust is not about ignoring our struggles; it's the belief that we are not alone, the conviction that we will be supported when we falter.

We come into this world knowing how to let go. As infants, our life is about total dependency. We are carried and coddled. Yet, we are wired to move past this stage, asserting our autonomy, pushing back, standing our own ground. We need this. We also need to know we can ask for help, feel safe, and loosen our grip. Somewhere in the transition from dependence to independence, it gets harder to let go.

Standing in that row of women waiting to cross the street, I was running through my mental to-do list. *Get it done, get it done,* was my internal drumbeat at that time (and admittedly, many other times as well). Then that magic sippy cup fell, and I was reminded…it's OK to let go and even experiment with how things tumble. That child could let go because Mom was there. I can too, when I remember G-d is right beside me.

A practice in trust begins with experimenting with loosening our grip on what we call reality. It can be as simple as lengthening the exhalation of our breath to feel what it's like to physically relax. It can be delegating a task, relinquishing control, and trusting another. Sometimes, it's trying out something new—an idea or a recipe—and releasing ourselves from the pressure of "getting it right." Each time we practice trusting, we inch a drop closer to G-d and build our capacity to navigate challenges.

That Mom had no idea how helpful she was. She was talking about *her kid,* but she was talking *to me.* Maybe she was talking to you too.

*"I trust G-d to defend me; He rescues those whose hearts are true."*
*(Tehillim 7:11)*

Having made it through a somewhat lengthy flight, a few patches of turbulence, and the usual in-flight announcements, we were making a smooth descent. In the night sky the city lights were growing larger, the pressure in my ears was mounting, and the excitement of almost being there was building. That is, until my seatmate quipped, "We're going the wrong way." A range of responses might have been appropriate in this scenario:

- "How do you know this?"
- "Are we not actually landing at our destination?"
- "What do you mean?"

I went with the latter. She motioned out the window. "We *were* going down…but *now* we are going back up!" The wrong way indeed. My mind went scrambling for answers. In the way we tell ourselves stories to make sense of our reality, I created a quick play-by-play of the last five minutes: The pilot had announced we were a precious seven minutes ahead of schedule, the seat-belt signs went on, we began our descent. The runway must not have been clear—we were too early, and thus would need to circle so we could land at the originally scheduled time. My cognitive accommodation lasted but a few moments, as the speaker system came on with the pilot announcing that a warning light had gone on atop one of the wings, and that some sort of maintenance procedure would be required before landing, and of course, there was "no need to worry."

Right. No need to worry. Enter anxiety, stage left. We were informed that we might see some action on the wings before we made our safe descent. I peered out and then wondered aloud whether they would indeed have told us had there been a need to worry.

Flying fears run the gamut from the "landlocked with fear" to the "get on board cuz it's safer than a car" mentality. I'm closer to the "easy flier" side of things. There is almost a delightful in-flight surrender, knowing that no matter how hard I grip the seat or peer out the window, I'm simply not in control. Even turbulence is fairly tolerable, as long as I know it's part of the ride.

We could really extend this to most life experiences. Knowing that the task is simply to stay hydrated, make the most of the time, and stretch every so often, makes trusting the journey pretty doable.

Until, that is, someone or something makes us think, *We're going the wrong way.*

When events, people, or conversations take an unexpected turn, we might initially tell ourselves a story to make sense of it; we find ways to believe that things will still be OK. But sometimes we get trust fatigue. We start to disconnect, and the way we found hope and tolerated the turbulence begins to lose its power. Then someone—like the pilot, a friend, or a well-meaning acquaintance—tells us, "No need to worry." And we think, *Really?! Are you kidding? How can I not worry?!*

We wonder if we really *are* going the wrong way; we begin to doubt ourselves and our capacity to endure. As our panic grows, we look around us for reassurance or simply a way out. What we miss when we are frantically looking for an escape route, is that the experience itself, the challenges along the way, aren't *in* the way, they *are* the way. Sometimes, the only way to the other side is through. When we face our fears and step into our challenges, we can move beyond them.

As for the flight landing, there really was no need to worry. I couldn't see much action on the wing, but in a few minutes, we made a safe landing. What looked like "going the wrong way" was simply an unexpected ascent along the route. As a passenger, my job was indeed to stay calm. I needed to trust that the delay, or the plane's ascent, was needed to ultimately arrive. Not always a simple feat. Even with reassurance, I was a little worried. All the more so in our lives.

I'm not suggesting we can completely rid ourselves of fear. It's more about looking at the bumpy landings and the "wrong way" moments and building trust in the journey, whispering gently to our anxious thoughts, "It's OK, you're not alone, this is part of the course." When we do that, we may just find that what looked so bad, what seemed so discouraging, was actually bringing us closer to our goal. If anxiety moves us away from G-d and our essence, trust can draw us closer.

I could tolerate that flight because I had a feeling that the pilot could be trusted. We can endure the unexpected when we trust in G-d as *The* Pilot. This doesn't make us passive passengers in life. How we react and who we become is our responsibility; choosing to trust and remain connected *is* within our control. Feeling the bumpy landing that late evening I was relieved, I was tired, but I also felt a deeper sense of security that I was *not* going the wrong way.

*"There is no joy like the resolution of doubts."*
(Metzudas Dovid, Mishlei 15:30)

I can't tell you exactly how it happened, but it did.

One morning I woke up, and there it was.

A group of kids had been playing in our backyard. Among the play apparatus was a ball inserted in a two-foot sleeve of colorful fabric. The players were whipping this toy around—watching its arc and catching it from all sorts of directions. That is, until one volley sent it on a journey with no return. It launched high up into the towering backyard tree, wrapping its multicolor tail around a branch and parking itself there with no way to get down.

For days afterward, we walked by the tree, noted the ball, and wondered how we'd ever get it down. This was no task to be completed with an average ladder. The limb was out of reach. There could be no branch-shaking rescue mission for our ball. It seemed pretty hopeless.

It's not even that I wanted that ball back so badly. We were doing just fine without it. It was, however, a bit of an eyesore brightly lodged up there. Bottom line: I really had no idea how, or if ever, we would get it down. And that's when it happened. I woke up, looked outside, and it was on the grass, gracefully reclining on the lawn beneath our tree.

How had it happened? A squirrel on the branch? The wind? A take-your-ball-down-from-the-tree fairy? It was irrelevant. What had been stuck was dislodged. The reality in the backyard had shifted—right when we thought it was impossible.

More than toys stuck in trees, challenges have a way of seeming simply unsolvable. We try to stretch ourselves to meet the challenge, but we give up or despair because we can't fathom it working out. From our limited perspective we don't see a resolution, so we give up on there being a solution at all.

Identifying our own self-doubt is the key to freedom, because it reminds us that there *is* a way out—we are not as stuck as we think. To believe we have no choice is a choice itself. Realizing this allows us to begin uncoiling the self-limiting beliefs wound up in our minds. When we see that there is more than one resolution to our challenges, we can better accept life's unexpected plot twists. We don't need to panic when we trust that another path or choice will likely present itself.

And that's where my backyard saga continues. Because once that ball-with-a-tail was free, it was not too long before it was relaunched into arboreal prison. Yes. It got thrown, and stuck, in another branch. But this time, I was less puzzled—or perhaps less doubtful—that it would find its way down. Since I had once experienced the joy of seeing it find its way home, I could trust that the ball—like so many pieces of my life—would find its proper place at exactly the right time.

Then there was that time I nearly walked off with someone else's gift basket. I thought it was mine, but it wasn't.

It was late at night. Travel weary, I checked into my hotel and made my way to my room. Deep breath, exhale. You know the feeling when you finally hear the click-close of the door, everything is quiet, you are alone. Nowhere left to go.

My hotel-room bliss was rudely interrupted by the realization that I had forgotten something and needed to return to the lobby. Elevator down and back to the front desk I went. "Ma'am, did you get your welcome gift basket?" the concierge asked.

"Um, no," I replied, somewhat puzzled. This was a nice hotel, but a gift basket?

"There's something for me?" Yes. It was confirmed.

The concierge began to head to the back to retrieve my welcome gift, but then paused. "You are here with the wedding party, right?" My excitement came to a full stop. There was nothing for me.

"No." Shucks. It's not like I'd *needed* the free basket, but once it was offered…well, I was excited. I mean, who can't get jazzed about an unexpected basket of goodies?

"Funny," she explained, "there's a group here for a wedding, and there's another guest with the same last name as you." Amusing indeed, along with disappointing. Something about the offer had me thinking that I actually *deserved*, even *needed* that gift basket.

I was able to collect myself and make it back to my room. But not without first joking, "I'll take it anyway." We shared a laugh. We all know this scenario is (literally) peanuts, but it's not so far off from the pining we do for everything we think ought to be ours.

Sometimes the experience of almost-having is more painful than the status quo: the promising job interviews, the exciting dates, the if-only-it-had-been experiences. At times, harder than a delay is a brush with arriving where we long to be. When we think it's ours, and then we realize—it's not. It never was. In the brief time that we feel that this date is our match, or that we're going to get the job, we dream up an entire life. When we discover it's not going to materialize, we are bereft. As if it was already ours, we mourn the loss of a life we never had and lament the future that never was.

I could get over that gift basket without too much trouble, but it's more of a struggle when I think something ought to be mine. Sometimes the gift is in *not* getting what we'd like. We just can't see it in the moment. It's one thing to look back over ten years and see how it was: "So good that I didn't get into that school," or "So grateful I didn't marry the wrong guy." It's another to be able to look at the here-and-now disappointments and find the concealed good.

Life's challenges would be easier to accept if they came with a welcome card and wrapped in a bow. It would make our work here simpler; we'd be more inclined to see the silver lining. But we live in a world of hidden gifts. Our task is to become detectives searching out the opportunities in every near miss—finding the good wrapped in each rejection.

I am not saying this is effortless. Dealing with dashed dreams and unrealized hopes is harder than walking away from a gift basket. It takes courage to say, "This isn't mine. It never was." It requires herculean efforts to gather a broken heart and believe we will love again. When we do, we create a tiny opening in ourselves, a little space to trust in G-d. The thing about the end of a relationship or an unmet goal is that it leaves room for someone or something else. Not necessarily what we'd expected, but neither are gift baskets. It's the surprise contents that delight us. Maybe we can discover a little bit of that wonder when it appears in our lives.

There really is no telling when the gifts will show up. If we keep our eyes open looking for the disguised gift baskets, we will find the Almighty sending us goodies along the way. The challenge is to see that whatever we find is exactly what we need—even when we need to let it go.

Like most bandwagon fans, I became a baseball enthusiast some-where toward the end of September a couple years back. Though my home team, the Toronto Blue Jays, enjoyed a brief spotlight in my youth, they were off my radar for the last couple of decades. All of that changed with a city swept by Blue Jay fever, myself among the newly baseball-concerned. My enthusiasm fits into the category my Bubby would have described as, "You live long enough, you see everything."

So, chapter two of sports fanhood began this spring. I'd be driving, listening to the news, and it would come to the sports report. Then, instead of tuning out, I'd tune in. As if the names of players and "RBIs" actually had relevance to me. Shocking. Well, at least to me. Then, I was ready to take it to the next level—in person attendance at a game. Yup. There I was, streaming into the Rogers Centre with thousands of eager fans. You can imagine, I saw a lot of life-lesson material there. The excitement. The unity. The common purpose. I was hooked. There was a unique thrill in watching the players, live, before my eyes.

The following day, I replayed the game in my mind, mulling over what had made it so exhilarating. What was it about sitting in the stands watching each play live, in real time, as it happened, that made me feel so excited? It had been somewhere in the bottom of the eighth when the ball sailed toward the outfield. We cheered. We hoped. Would it be caught? Would it be a home run? Between the hope and the uncertainty was the very place of excitement. Somewhere wrapped into the I-don't-know-how-this-is-going-to-go was the pleasure itself. The delight we felt was in witnessing the unknown arc of the ball. In truth, I don't even remember what happened. Was it a run or an out? The result was secondary to the witnessing itself.

In that moment, we let go of needing to *know* the outcome (though the wished-for direction was clear) and instead, leaned into watching it unfold. I couldn't help but wonder: *What would it be like if we could show up to life in the same way?* Can you imagine if, in the midst of a day/meeting/job interview/date, we could relinquish control, and similarly marvel at the process unfolding? Somewhere between hope and uncertainty is this magical feeling: an excited sense of trust.

We live in the shadow world where people, places, and yes, even baseball games, are all hints at the true world of the soul. Our job is to seek out the way the Almighty operates within the laws of nature. If a curveball (in life or on the field) is thrown our way, we don't need to get caught up in the play itself. The thrill of being a fan in the stands is possible because when all is said and done, we know our basic sense of self and security does not hinge on that game. We will return to our lives. I can't expect to look at my life with the same gleeful detachment. But maybe I can learn a little bit from my aspiring fanhood.

I imagine playing on the field is less relaxing than watching from the stands. It's likely that the players don't feel as excited by the uncertainty of the game, because they feel the stress and pressure of winning. We likewise stand on the field of our lives, trying to micromanage reality and control the outcome. Efforts are in our control, results belong to G-d. We are expected to put in maximal, reasonable efforts, all the while recognizing that the Almighty takes care of the outcome. When we live with that consciousness, the uncertainty is less scary; there is less need to hold our breath and more room to delight in the unfolding.

Baseball is, at times, more exciting than my uncertain future, but when I recall the thrill of being at that game, I can embrace some of the unknown. I still stumble into attempts to control and stress about the future, but sometimes I can let go and trust that my life is unfolding—and *that* is truly worth cheering about.

*"In the day, when I am afraid, I will put my trust in You."*

(*Tehillim 56:4*)

Eleanor Roosevelt is credited with saying that you should "do one thing every day that scares you." It was in this vein of stepping out of my comfort zone and trying something new that I was hitting golf balls at a driving range, all in the name of "fun." Let me say, there is nothing fun about stooping over to try (and retry) balancing a small, white ball on a tiny white peg...and then watching it roll off before even attempting to hit it.

A putting green neophyte, I was willing to take it all in stride, breathe deeply, keep my eye on the ball, and bear my own sense of incompetence. Swing, miss, swing, miss was my rhythm for quite a while.

And then, the miracle happened. My club made contact with the ball. There was movement. Which direction? How far? I didn't care. The simple experience of effecting a change, a trajectory, was pure exhilaration! Then I found my swing. More and more, the club was connecting with the ball. The sound of contact registered with equal surprise—and then I would watch in wonder. Where would it go? How far? How high? My part was the set-up, the swing, and then—letting go of the need to control the outcome, surrendering to curiosity and wonder.

With so much of life spent working toward accomplishment, it is liberating to stand in unskilled territory. The prerequisites are as simple as they are challenging: be willing to feel scared and get ready for some discomfort.

Stepping out of our comfort zone, as a daily practice, obviously makes us more vulnerable than putting greens and golf balls gone afield. But it's a way of building trust—in ourselves and in G-d. Doing something every day that scares us teaches us that we don't need to be good at something to make the effort worthwhile, and that *we* are worthwhile without being good at everything. We are loveable in our learning selves, i.e., the parts of us that are imperfect, unknowing, and even fearful. Each day that G-d gifts us ratifies this reality. Each breath we take is a confirmation of our worthiness. Even if we fall, even in the messy parts of ourselves, the Almighty is lovingly holding us up.

When we feel this love, we can take risks and don't need to hold on so tight—we are supported. Knowing this, failure stops being the enemy as we come to trust that whatever happens, we *can* regroup and recover. Our power is in our reaction; our choice is to learn and find the willingness to be vulnerable. We will do this work in that magical place—a tiny step beyond the familiar.

When we live this way, we see that our job is not to control every outcome and avoid imperfection, but rather it's to learn and grow. How do we get there? By entering the space between what we know and what we have yet to discover.

Our world is full of these opportunities. One of my favorite situations is trying to get into difficult parking spots. I'm serious. I savor these mini moments of discomfort. Maybe yours is speaking up where you usually stay silent or taking up a new hobby. It requires courage to say, "I'm willing to do this, with all its uncertainty. Even when it scares me."

I don't pretend to be able to always live this way. But I do know, as surely as I am certain that I will never be a pro golfer, that it's a daily practice. Moment-to-moment willingness can bring us a step closer to a reality where fear is transformed into trust. It requires a life committed to being honest about the days when I am afraid, and from that place believing that however this turns out, wherever the golf balls of life land, I will be OK.

Who knew that a GPS is also a travel log? I hadn't seen it quite that way—until last week. I needed to go somewhere. I knew the general location but needed a GPS to get there. I opened up the Waze app on my phone, recalling that I'd been to this spot last year. And so, the hunt for the address began: scrolling down and down until I found it at the bottom of almost a year's worth of travels. The Niagara Falls Rainbow Bridge, a national park in Iceland, and a factory outlet address were among the landings I had made. If you were to ask me about the past several months, I might recount the ups and downs—the way my days were filled—but I'm not sure I'd give you a list of locations. But here it was: my life in geography, my story told in addresses. In a world that calls upon us to define ourselves by what we do or who we've become, this timeline suggested another way to look at life.

We build monuments in time. We visit and revisit the cycle of the year—each time anew, and yet always bearing the mark of previous years. For example, each birthday is a new event, but we likewise experience it through the lens of every previous birthday. When we celebrate, we are not simply marking a date; we are encountering the energy we call "birthday." So too with festivals and seasons, as we cycle through the year, each point in time emanates from the past, is lived in the present, and informs the future. There will never be another moment like this, but it will be influenced by all that has come before. So too our travels become the story of where we've been—and where we are headed.

If my Waze was letting me retrace my steps, it also caused me to wonder: *Which address might be next?* I once asked a teacher who has inspired countless people with his writing and teaching, "Twenty years ago, could you have imagined where your life would be today?"

"No," he replied, "and I can't wait to see what the next twenty years will bring."

This was revolutionary to me: he was excited by the uncertainty! He trusted that just as the Almighty had guided him toward unexpected greatness, the story would continue to unfold with Divine guidance. The need was not to know how or when, but simply to trust in the process itself. If Waze has anything to tell us, it is that yet-unknown addresses will find their way into our spiritual GPS.

It's easy to trust when we play with a metaphor or look back on our travels. Hindsight is twenty-twenty because, on the other side of our experiences, we see that somehow we survived. The real skill lies in setting off on a journey, plodding through midway, and believing that we will get to where our souls need to go. Scrolling through our lives will reveal a mixture of triumphs and setbacks, moments we'd be happy to capture and those we'd rather edit out of our personal travel log.

The call of the future contains both a promise and a challenge: we *will* get there, but *where* that is is beyond our knowing. What *is* within our control is how we engage with the process and our attitude toward the journey. Can we embrace the uncertainty, trusting that the destinations ahead will be perfectly planned for our soul?

Our task is to scan our past for evidence that each experience was indeed for our ultimate good. While not necessarily easy or desired, struggles we somehow survived prove that we are resilient. When we gather this sense about our personal history, we can show up to the present with more confidence and look to the future with greater trust.

I don't know which addresses I'll put into my Waze next. Who really does? If the past has any forecast on the future, there will be twists and turns and unexpected detours. For now I'm trying to let go of needing to know and embrace the uncertainty. I might even get to the point of saying with excitement, "I can't wait to see what the next twenty years will bring."

I saw the train entering the station. I was at the top of the escalator with two eager ten-year-olds. Had I been traveling solo, I would have made a dash for it, likely sliding in as the doors began to close. But contemplating the challenge of all three of us making it down quickly, I calculated, was more than I was up for. I pictured something of a rough-and-tumble event on the escalator, and calmly told my inner rushing-voice, "Go slowly, another train will come."

We landed on the platform as the train left the station. The girls expressed their disappointment, but I was already armed with a silver-lining answer, pointing to the screen that predicted the next train arriving in four minutes. And it did. After four minutes, the subway slid into the station and we hopped on board, finding our seats.

Then we waited. And waited. No movement. Then came the crackle of the PA system. This could only mean one thing: a delay. Fine, all part of the public transit experience. But here the plot thickens—we were informed that a fire crew had been dispatched to the station ahead, and they would let us know more as information became available. I was far less excited than the girls. An emergency call can mean a lot of things, and fire crews are rarely there because of an actual fire. The clock continued to tick. Two seats over, a woman looked up from her phone and shared with those in earshot, "A friend of mine is texting me. She's walking outside the next station. She says there is a commotion over there." People started to trickle off the subway. We soon followed suit, somewhat deflated, as the transit personnel announced it would be at least another thirty-minute delay.

It wasn't until we had returned home that we heard the radio report. The train had indeed caught fire, filling with smoke as its passengers evacuated. Later, I read how people had been led on foot through the dark subway tunnels to safety. Reports said no one was injured on board that train.

A few more rushed steps and our story would have been very different. I would be sharing a much more dramatic tale than a simple saga of subway delays. I'd likely also have had a couple of very shaken girls emerging from their underground adventure. Or, had we been five minutes earlier, we would've been on a train *before* the fire started. We would have made our way downtown and likely thought little of the miracle of timing that carried us there.

Without a glitch in our plans, we simply think things are running as they should. No miracles. Just us doing our thing. Right? Without clear reminders that G-d is involved in every detail of lives, it's easy to forget.

Most of the time, we don't see the near misses. We live in the dark, or the illusion that we know what's coming next. I mentally run through my day as I brush my teeth in the morning. One of my favorite mother-daughter conversations is detailing our plans for the week ahead.

But all of that hinges on things playing out as we expect. And here is the truth: because most of the time we don't see behind the scenes, we miss out on seeing how miraculous every bit really is.

I suppose it would have made a more exciting story if we'd actually been evacuated. But we'd also have missed the chance to wonder: How often does Hashem guide us, keep us safe, and direct us through our challenges without us knowing? Our wiser soul-selves may say, "Always," but in the moment, we don't always see it that way. The experiences we have that show us His Divine guidance are opportunities to build our trust that—even when it's not so clear—G-d is lovingly directing our lives.

For now, we are left to dream of a time when it will always be as clear as that missed train, when reality will be filled with soul-awareness and G-d consciousness. We may have been delayed along our subway journey, but for a short while, we fast-tracked our knowledge of Hashem. For that, I'd get stuck on the subway all over again.

## YOUR TURN: GUIDE QUESTIONS

- Can you look throughout your day for signs of G-d's kindness and presence? Could you experiment with a daily practice of recording where you see the Almighty in your life? Every time we do this, we build our muscles of trust.
- What is an experience you have had where in hindsight, you see that Hashem was taking care of you? Can you look at today and trust that Hashem is likewise guiding you on this part of your journey?
- What is one way you can step outside of your comfort zone today? Is it reaching out to someone? Trying a new experience? Driving a different route? There are small ways we can build our capacity to take risks and feel secure in the process.
- What is an area of your life you feel you try to control or over-function in? Can you try asking Hashem for help in that area and remind yourself that G-d is in control of the outcome?

# CHAPTER 5
# Purpose

"The first gate is that a person working on himself should
know his value: his level, and his greatness, and his
importance, and how beloved he is to his Creator."
(*Rabbeinu Yonah, Shaarei Teshuvah*)

*"The soul that You, my G-d, have given me is pure. You created it, You
formed it, You breathed it into me, You protect it within me…"*
(*Birchos Hashachar*)

I t was as if I knew her. She came into the restaurant pushing a shopping
cart like a walker. Her velour tracksuit and large turquoise clip-on earrings
matched her well-coiffed hairdo. The blush streaked across her cheeks
hinted to a time gone by when she had surely been a youthful beauty.

As she sat down at the table next to us, I was nothing short of tickled. I
must admit that due to my innate curiosity, one of my dining challenges
is staying focused on who I'm with at a restaurant. Not that present
company wasn't appreciated, but the sideshow setting up to my left was
terrific. Across from her sat a young woman.

"The food is really excellent here," she confided to her young companion.
The waiter came to their table. The older lady ordered fish and chips, "Extra
hot, extra crispy. That's how I like it." I think she even winked at him.

She wanted to know why there wasn't bread and butter on the table.
It wasn't a demand, nor was it a simple inquiry. She asked in the way the
old can: while offering commentary on how things ought to be, she made
her needs known. Fresh rolls, "Just for you, ma'am," soon arrived.

The conversation in earshot continued, including her plans for the upcoming week (bridge at the community centre) and how much she loved the restaurant food. I was in heaven. While we were strangers, there was a delicious familiarity to the scene. I had once sat at that table, treated to a similar lunch date with my own Bubby.

So you won't be surprised that I found an opportunity to strike up a conversation with her lunch date as we both waited in line at the cash register. If five minutes could yield life-in-a-short-biography, I got it. Esther, ninety-eight years old. Lives on her own. Daughter in LA, grandson in San Francisco. Don't seem to visit much. She is hardheaded. Fired every home care nurse she's had. A die-hard Miami Heat fan. Doesn't miss a game. Soft spot for popcorn. And her companion? A neighbor from her building. Checks in on her, takes her to basketball games. Brings groceries. They all do. The neighbors, that is. They take turns taking care of Esther.

Last week this neighbor came by with some milk. Esther wanted to pay her for it. She wouldn't hear of it. "Fine," she countered. "I'll take you for lunch next week." And here we were, at the lunch-date-for-milk rendezvous. But what neither party knew was that they were likewise treating me; not to a meal, but a much deeper experience.

I can't begin to tell you how much pleasure those two women gave me. Maybe it's because Esther reminded me so much of my Bubby, a woman who never left the house without lipstick, and ordered her pizza, "Well-done and extra hot." Perhaps it was the relationship between the two and knowing that a whole floor of neighbors loves her. But I think the greatest joy was simply being in the presence of a woman no longer concerned with being anyone other than herself.

As the bread arrived, she remarked with gusto, "I like bread." Her arthritic, bent fingers were bedazzled with rings. There was no apologizing for who she was. Being in the presence of a woman so wholly herself has a way of leaving some fairy dust in its wake; as if we might also let go a little of the everyday anxiety of becoming ourselves to simply be. Granted, she's had ninety-eight years of practice. I imagine she has had her own struggles in life, and still does. But they are no longer about knowing her value. Perhaps a healthy sense of entitlement is the gift of verging on one hundred years old, but it can also come when we identify with our soul selves.

Knowing that we are a work in progress also means that we are simultaneously exactly as we ought to be. Something about that lunch date left me with a bounce in my step and a smile on my face. Esther's way of being permeated me. I was accurate when I said that it was as if I knew her. I do. It is the clarity within that G-d has created my soul. Formed it. Breathed it into me. So, next time you see her—that piece of your soul that knows it is whole—smile. You might just find her smiling back at you.

It's probably a conversation you've had many times. Technology is good. Technology is bad. We are more connected than ever. We are more distracted than ever. We love our phones. We love to hate our phones. It was during one of these debates that a techy friend asked, "Do you actually know the definition of technology?" I didn't. "It's the practical application of science." That's it. No mention of wires or Wi-Fi.

"So basically, a potato peeler fits the bill?" I asked. Yes, my friend confirmed. It's practical, it's applied, and there is science to it. Yet, none of us are anxious about peelers shortening attention spans or interrupting dinner. Defining our terms changed our conversation. While iPhones and artificial intelligence might be infiltrating our lives, most kitchen utensils aren't threatening the fabric of society. That's where definitions become important. They help us know what we are working with. When we grasp what is meant by a given term or idea, we create a common language and a deeper understanding.

I recall a professor telling my class of eager undergrads during a lecture on essay writing: "You have to define your terms." Wise words. We were being coached in the realm of making arguments, thinking clearly, and communicating our point. "Whose definition are you using? What are the words representing?" He was also telling us to say what we mean. "Don't use jargon. Don't hide behind fancy words. Figure out what you are talking about. It's not about falling in love with the dictionary or getting into fancy verbiage. In fact, it's the opposite. It means coming down from overthinking and describing to find the clear point we are trying to make." This isn't only needed when writing a paper or debating the value of technology (potato peelers included)—it's the stuff of life. Communication hinges on this clarity. We've all shown up in the wrong place for a meeting (oh, you meant *that* Starbucks) or had our words painfully misunderstood. Shared language makes relationships possible. Shared definitions makes them magical.

Yes, we need to articulate to others, but defining our terms is most importantly about ourselves. If we are to build our lives based on values, we need to know what they are. We can't stay at the level of labels like "honesty," "truth," and "love." They are good beginnings. Our job is to ask, "What does that mean? What are the working concepts of my life? What am I about?" We need to define these in terms that are simple and functional. When we have this clarity, we are able to communicate our values. We can say to our kid, "Being honest means telling the truth even when we don't like it"; or explain to a colleague, "Being honest means I report all my income." The meaning of honesty is different at home and in business, as are the actions we take.

The clearer we are about our terms, the more they will fuel and guide our choices. I might explain to a friend that, "spiritual growth means I'm willing to be uncomfortable if that's what it takes to listen to my soul, my higher self, over my body." When I'm not feeling so spiritual or in the mood to grow, remembering those words can help me reconnect to my spiritual goals.

If we are clear about the definitions of our values, then in times of stress, we can stick to them. This is a struggle. The work of gaining clarity is not reserved for essays. It's easy to edit down a piece or debate the merits of technology. It takes some grit to look for wisdom and find clarity. I'm glad we have potato peelers. I am also grateful for that professor. They both remind me that it's worth the hard work.

*"If you have seized a lot, you have not seized."*

*(Yoma 80a)*

I have a passion for dollar stores. Back in the days of my youth, a dollar store was a corner mom-and-pop outfit with odds and ends: a few rubber balls, poor quality toys, and other "where in the world do they make this stuff?" items. But the landscape of single-digit purchasing has changed, with entire chains devoted to selling items manufactured far away to entice their consumers.

Now, the discerning shopper will know—there are certain items that are, well, er, best *not* to buy in one of these establishments. Adhesives tend to be weaker, colors have a way of running, and toys have a penchant for falling apart, often before the packaging has made its way to the trash.

But oh, the items that we *can* buy. All too easily, a trip to the dollar store becomes a trip to the fifty-dollar store. That cart becomes full of *stuff*. These are things I clearly *need*, like cheerful napkins, a twenty-pack of pens, tinfoil pans and a stack of craft supplies, not to mention the super cute vases and shockingly cheap notebooks. It was in such a state that I found myself pulling out my wallet and marveling at all I was about to purchase at the checkout, while wondering in the back of my mind, *Do I really need all this? Will it actually get used? Where will it go?*

Grabbing all that stuff in the heat of "Can you believe it costs only a dollar?!" has a way of seducing us into grabbing more than we need—perhaps even more than we care to contend with upon getting home. It is ever so tempting to likewise fill our shopping carts of life with more, newer, updated. The latest craze, a better way—these tend to contribute to goals set too high and hopes scattered madly off in all directions. It's not that we set out to overfill our days, but like well-intentioned trips to the dollar store, our schedules can get jammed without our even noticing it. Voices that taunt us with "How can you say no?" or "Just one more thing" can lead us to the checkout of life with a bill we simply cannot manage.

We may realize that we were overzealous in trying to do it all and ask, "What does not actually belong in my life at this moment?" It requires an honest look at all we have committed to and extended ourselves toward and a focus on what we really want to keep carrying. If we don't prioritize our lives, someone else will. As victims of multitasking and people pleasing, we will end up spread thin and burnt out. The irony is that by trying to do it all, our energy is diffused and we end up less effective.

Just like dollar store shopping, the temptation to grab a lot can leave us empty handed. It's time we gave ourselves permission to empty out our carts down to the essentials. This isn't to say we won't return to the tasks we've "shelved," only that we will reconsider them when our "cart" is less full.

Getting clarity on the few things we actually *can* accomplish—zeroing in on them and committing to doing them well—is about as exciting as removing the sparkly dollar store item from my basket, i.e., a total buzzkill. But the aftermath—the lightened load and the ability to comfortably carry those items home and put them away with ease—is worth every moment of surrender. It may entail ignoring the voices calling out, "Buy me!" "Say yes!" and, "You have to accept this opportunity," if the time isn't right.

Overextending ourselves may not lead us, pulling out our wallet, to the cash register, but it can leave us spiritually destitute. Figuring out what we truly want to fill our lives with, and focusing—little by little—leads to incremental gains and true growth. We can find the courage to say no to the committee and yes to our kids. We can learn the art of declining an invitation in favor of much-needed rest.

The gift of a life where we respect our limitations and honor our priorities is that it's filled with what is most important to us. So that next time we are tempted to offer an impulsive yes (dollar store purchases included), we might pause and ask: *What do I really want to really hold on to?*

**"Who is rich? One who is satisfied with his lot."**

*(Pirkei Avos 4:1)*

Missing a package delivery is like finding fairy dust on your pillow: evidence that something is waiting for you somewhere, but it's not here. I had returned home to a postal love note, aka, one of those notes hanging from the doorknob stating that I'd missed a delivery and could pick it up at the postal office. The note was addressed to my last name, and a somewhat intelligible first initial. I didn't recall ordering anything and began to wonder:

Was it actually addressed to *me*?

What *was* it?

Would it still be there when I showed up?

The sense that something is waiting—and we may have missed it—has a way of leaving its own kind of not-so-fairy-like dust in our lives. We look at other peoples' successes and believe that they could have been our own. We say no to a date and then when we hear he's engaged, worry that he should have been "*my* husband." We look at a friend's job, kids, house, marriage, and think, "I'd do better—I would know how to really appreciate that life." This perspective usually starts with sentences like, "It's not fair," or "If I had realized then..." These thoughts coat our days with regret, as if a different life and soul purpose could have been ours—*but we missed it*. If only we'd shown up sooner, chosen differently, or done more. We fear that we are missing out.

The problem with this, "if only" mentality is that we *do* miss out. We miss what's right in front of us. Lusting after other people's lives or anxiously adding more stuff to our own diffuses our energy and prevents us from focusing on what we have. Feeling like we don't *have* enough is driven by a deeper fear: that we *aren't* enough.

With this feeling of lack, we get ourselves into trouble, making choices guided by fear. We are driven to fill this void, grabbing every opportunity while hoping that "this will be the thing that completes me." We anxiously pile more on our plate or pine after the "one who got away," yet all the while what we *do* have is vying for our attention. Like a young child frantically trying to be noticed, our life tugs at us, begging that we see more of what we have and less of what we are missing.

Focusing on missed opportunities robs us of our present lives. Our work is to cultivate the certainty that what we have and who we are *is* enough. I didn't say complete or as we'd like, I said enough. Which means looking at the gaps and yes, even missed opportunities, as exactly what we need to accomplish the unique mission of our soul. We don't need someone else's career, kids, or house to do the job of being us. In fact, those things would likely get in the way. Once we have this clarity, *then* we can make choices about the next step, what to add and what we ought to remove. It's easier to show up to the party of our own lives than it is to constantly worry about everything we are missing.

In case you are hanging in suspense...the item *was* addressed to me. It was my new passport. I had missed the delivery but got it from the post office instead. I hadn't missed my chance after all. If second chances come for travel documents, all the more so when it comes to the passport of our soul. We will get snagged in "if only" thinking, we will get derailed by worry over lost opportunities; but we will likewise be given the chance to come back and pick up where we left off. That's the shared kindness of the earthly and Heavenly postal service: the package is waiting, our mission is available to us. We just need to pick it up and carry on with what we've already got.

Sometimes I wish I could use Google to ask my big life questions. Imagine if you could use Google Scholar to pull up peer-reviewed articles advising your next life move? Can you imagine typing in your latest conundrum, clicking on the search button, and finding a flurry of links with personalized direction and the answers you've been seeking? Perhaps they'd call it Google Soul. Imagine the business ventures based on this function, Silicon Valley hard at work, all vying for your spiritual search to come zooming into headquarters.

Google Soul might be more fantasy than reality, but I'm not sure we're far off the mark. We want answers and that's a good thing. A craving for clarity and direction is a sign of spiritual health. This desire for understanding is the rumbling of our soul pointing us on a journey. The challenge is that we expect the results to come as quickly as high-speed Wi-Fi. Our work in this life is to engage in the search.

When we long for answers, we are tapping into a spiritual yearning. If we use that yearning to seek meaning and G-d, we are fulfilling our mission, which might mean redefining our mission to one less focused on the outcome and more committed to the searching itself. As important as the answer is how we find it. It's through this process that we cultivate an understanding of who we are, what we most want, and how G-d is calling to us in our lives. If we are too wrapped up in getting to the end, we miss out on all that can be gleaned through the finding.

For the internet neophyte, a basic search can feel awkward. A spiritual search can feel equally uncomfortable when we first start out or enter a new phase. When we sense something missing from our lives or struggle with big questions, it's a charge to start looking.

Google might have us all fooled into thinking that results come quickly, but soul work can't be rushed. Finding Hashem winking throughout our day requires more than typing a few words. In essence, it's an ongoing mindfulness exercise where we bring awareness to the present moment and look for G-d in the details.

When looking for the Divine becomes a moment-by-moment practice, then every cup of coffee, breath of air, annoying email, and beat of my heart is a chance to feel the Divine in the day to day. We can't use Google Soul, but we can train ourselves to see the hints in our own lives. When we live within search mode, we are in an active relationship with our Creator.

The conversation shifts from a perfunctory request to an intimate dialogue. Like in any relationship, there are times of closeness and periods of distance. The fundamental shift is that our questions help us come closer—searching out the Divine pulls us into a deeper connection. From a place of connection, we can listen more carefully for the ways G-d is guiding us and providing hints to our personal mission.

It doesn't mean that every moment is effortless, or that the messages are what we desire...but it does create a life where no matter where we are, however big the questions we face, there is always meaning in our quest.

*"I lift up my eyes to the mountains—from where does my help come?*
*My help comes from Hashem, the Maker of heaven and earth."*
(Tehillim 121:1–2)

Amid a flurry of emails, work deadlines, and real-time family needs, "Table Topics" brought me great solace.

Table Topics is a neat little set of cards, described on the box as, "Questions to start great conversations." One of these cards asks the question: "If you could live either by the water or by the mountains, which would you choose?"

My usual answer? Water. No question about it. The sound of the waves, the movement before my eyes, and the chance to swim are all top reasons why I would choose water.

That was all until the Table Topics card reminded me of the value of the mountains. While the water still calls to me, a few other calls I received had me re-jigging my notion of what I need. It started with a barrage of requests to which I "couldn't say no." It continued with a flurry of stressful emails and late-night parenting challenges. You get the picture. The usual storm of life was brewing, and I had the feeling I'd rather run for cover. What I really needed to do was stand strong, draw boundaries, and remind myself that the stress winds of life won't knock me over.

Sometimes it's easy to hold the line, stand firm, or push back. Other times it's not. We each exist somewhere along this continuum. Our ability to stand strong sways as people and events complicate our day. We capitulate when the puppy-faced child begs for something and we feel our internal I'm-not-giving-in resolve crumble...or we say yes to being on a committee when we don't have the time or energy.

So, it was with some recent challenges that I started searching for the strength to set some limits. It would have been much easier to let go, say yes to that child's request for one more cookie, or passively give in to one more demand. It would take boundary-setting courage to hold a line. It was when I called deep for this courage that the Table Topics card reminded me of the wisdom of the mountain.

I recall learning that the power of the mountain is not in how it shakes its fists, sways with the wind, or moves about in the face of change—rather, it stays still. The mountain's power is in its ability to know where it needs to be and its role in the world. With this quiet greatness, it does not back down. So, I changed my Table Topics answer, because sometimes I need more mountain energy in my life.

I replied to that email kindly and firmly. I said yes to some requests and no to others. I still love the water, but I can learn so much from the mountain—we all can. So long as we are deeply rooted, standing in connection with our Creator, we can indeed hold those lines. Shaking fists and raised voices are the symptoms of fear and uncertainty. Compassionate limit setting is the legacy of mountain language in our lives. Clear boundaries allow us to live in line with our values and better focus our energy. When we can kindly say no where it's needed, we have more ability to say yes when it's important.

Sometimes we need to look to the mountains to make it through the day. When we do, we not only learn the lesson of quiet power and kind strength—we remind ourselves that we are being helped all along by the Maker of heaven and earth. This doesn't make life easy. Fear will creep in. We will question ourselves. That's OK; the mountain isn't going anywhere. Its lesson is there for us every day.

In the past thirty years, not much has changed about the tree in our backyard. At least, that's how it *seems*. A towering maple, it has become a landmark of sorts. In directing people to our home, I'll say, "Look for the large maple tree with a tire swing hanging from it." Many long summer afternoons have been spent climbing its branches; friends and neighbors have come to bask in its shade and use the swing.

Still, most days I walk past that tree and barely notice its presence. It's just there. The same. Each year, fall is signaled by the shedding of its leaves and every spring the maple keys dance in the air, signaling the long summer days ahead. Yet even in this cycle, there is consistency—with little variation.

As a teenager, I went away for the summer. I returned feeling changed by my travels and found it so disappointing that the tree seemed not to have grown or changed in my absence. As if its leaves should have turned multicolored or its trunk widened to reflect my expanded sense of the world. But it looked exactly as it had a couple months earlier before my own transformative experiences.

Over time, I have come to see the tree differently. What looked like sameness is actually stability—quiet, steady growth. Planted. Firm. It *is* developing...just in whispers, tiny movements—quiet greatness imperceptible to the untrained eye.

So much in life is unstable. Our health, finances, and dreams can come and go with little warning. Some days feel hopeful. Others make the task of putting one foot in front of the other on par with scaling Mount Everest. All the while, that tree just doesn't move. It has never—no matter how crabby, flighty, or anxious I have felt—gotten up and walked away. *That* is its greatness: the ability to stand strong and steady when the world is ever shifting. In a time when we value everything that is instant, quick, and innovative, it takes strength to simply be. The ability to stay fast to values, to remain true to our ideals in the face of adversity, pain, and challenge is the key to greatness. It is tempting to give in to the desires of the moment or the pressures of the day. Sometimes our job is simply to hold on.

We live in a world that begs for us to react, to always *do something*. It's easy to give in to this belief, particularly when we are emotionally depleted and physically run down. When we are hungry or tired or in need of some love, we often feel compelled to act, talk back, do something, *anything*, to make a change. The choices we make from this place are seldom based in wisdom and tend to lead us away from our goals. And then we have tree moments, the often unsung, private times when we stand strong. We keep going when it's hard, we pray despite disappointments, we steadfastly work toward a goal without seeing immediate results.

We can stand strong, be who we are, even when no one is cheering, because we, like that tree in my backyard, have roots firmly planted. We may have forgotten how deeply they run. That's OK. Discovering where we come from, exploring what nourishes our soul, and clarifying what we want to grow into, builds our root system.

We likely have moments and people in our lives who have been stable and held fast in the face of an ever-changing world. We may pass them by, and like that tree, mistake their apparent constancy for "not changing much." In truth, they stand for the quiet, whispered sort of heroics, because change, growth, and greatness, is often not a matter of appearances. It does not come in the form of multicolored maple leaves (much as my adolescent eyes may have craved such drama), but in the small acts and times when we remain connected to our purpose. Others may walk by us and think that not much has changed, but we know that it is in those quiet moments that we hear the whisper loudest, *Grow! Grow!*

Sometimes, just sometimes, we accept the invitation.

**"Hashem knows the days of the wholehearted..."**
*(Tehillim 37:18)*

"Be Amazing." If only it were that simple.

Those were the words printed upon a pillow on a chair at my workplace. I walked by this phrase so many times that it became part of the scenery. For some reason, on one sunny Monday afternoon, it caught my eye. Sweet, really. A pillow painted in rainbow stripes with the simple suggestion, "Be Amazing." A cheerful reminder of possibility.

Such statements of hope, cheerleading gestures and images coaxing us to dream, seem to abound these days. I think this particular item was purchased at a bookstore, wedged somewhere between mugs, stationary, and scarves (where *are* the books in bookstores these days?), this colorful item made its home upon an unsuspecting chair. Given the rough day I was having, I pondered how deceptively simple the phrase made it seem.

I imagined a scene where the pillow starts to shout at a world full of struggle and complexity: "Just be amazing!" Then the chair beneath it, the surface that has supported so many ever-so-real human beings, replies, "Sounds nice, but really? Life is harder than that. It's not so easy to be amazing with all of life's hardship. It's a cute saying, Mr. Pillow, but it's overly simplistic."

In reality, furniture isn't talking, and truth be told, I love such quotable quotes and cutesy house decor. I also didn't have long to stand and ponder, but it did start me wondering...could being amazing sometimes really be that simple—or that colorful?

The next day, when texting with a friend, the conversation went as follows:

Me: *How are you doing?*

Friend: *Life is a roller coaster. Trying to ride it and not fall off ;)*

Me: *Even if you fall off—you know how to get back on the ride*

Friend: *Just don't want to break any bones*

Me: *Good plan. Worst case = we get you a cast*

Friend: *Ya. A cast that I could paint*

And then I remembered that pillow. And all the colorful stripes behind the charge to "Be Amazing." Maybe this state of "amazingness" is about the way we paint the emotional breaks and bruises along the way.

And that's where the pillow gets it wrong: it's focused outward. The pillow is flashing with all its color, begging for attention. Sometimes we notice it, sometimes we walk right by. Not so different from our own bids for love and attention. We put an awful lot of effort into getting other people to tell us we are OK. We share photos and accomplishments, choose outfits and even careers, in pursuit of external validation. But perhaps there is pillow wisdom to be learned. Being amazing is about soft greatness and technicolor living, even if nobody notices. Our true value is about how we meet challenges in the personal moments of life. No applause. No accolades. Worthy in ourselves, without depending on other people to confirm our value.

It's possible to build a life and a character in deeply private ways: choosing our words carefully, anonymously helping a friend, pausing to talk to G-d. In those times, when we seemingly fade into the furniture of life, we may mistake going unrecognized by the world for being less than amazing.

Here is the thing I learned from that pillow: what might not be noticed, what we accomplish when nobody is watching, is one of the keys to greatness. Because that's when we define ourselves by what only we and Hashem know. Moments of unsung heroism are opportunities to practice this way of living, where we base our value on our private selves, inner character, and relationship to G-d.

When we catch ourselves in a secret success, we can learn to likewise validate our efforts. By naming and noting these accomplishments, we become our own personal cheerleaders. Learning to validate ourselves, we no longer need to outsource our worthiness and depend on the world to make us feel OK. It's an exercise in trusting that in the up and down of the journey, there is One Who sees our wholehearted attempts at everyday amazingness.

No doubt I will walk by that pillow again without taking much notice. It's also pretty likely we will each have moments where we step up to the challenges in our lives and gain some pretty awesome stripes—while no one is watching, loving, or applauding. That's where we get to "Be *Truly* Amazing."

## YOUR TURN: GUIDE QUESTIONS

- What are the key values that are guiding your life? If you had to choose three guiding principles in your life, what would they be? Make a goal each morning to focus on one way of living these values. Write them out and put them somewhere you can see them daily. Ask yourself at the end of each day: How have I been living these values? How can I do better tomorrow?

- What are the priorities in your life? Make a list of your priorities and how much time you spend each day devoted to them. Does your time match up with what is most important to you? Are there ways you want to change what you are doing? Next time someone asks you to do something, or an opportunity arises, ask yourself: Does this fit with what is most important to me?

- Where are you afraid to set boundaries? When is it hard for you to say no? How can you practice setting compassionate boundaries—loving someone by setting a limit?
- What are some of your more private accomplishments? Can you reward yourself for how you act when you're on your own, or how you manage things in the privacy of your home? Try setting a goal that only you will know about (maybe how you talk to your spouse, how patient you are with a child, or a commitment to connect to G-d). Make a chart for yourself—give yourself a check mark or a star every time you have a private success. This will build your own sense of worthiness, independent of what others see or how you are viewed.

CHAPTER 6

# Connection to G-d

"Your Presence, Hashem, do I seek…"

*(Tehillim 27:8)*

*"Take words with you and return to Hashem."*

*(Hoshea 14:2)*

"**D**id you remember to put a note in my lunch box?" Yup, *she's* reminding *me*. A little role reversal perhaps. Definitely a win. I started packing "Have a great day" notes when my daughter was in first grade. I come from a long line of note-writing, card-sending women, so I was all ready to follow suit. But when the lunch box would come home with the note still there, I wasn't sure it was noticed. I kept at it for a bit, undeterred by the lukewarm response. I mean, we don't parent like we're aiming for a five-star Trip Advisor rating. Now *that* would be interesting—can you imagine? Receiving a three-star review for dinner? A complete pan of your disciplinary measures? No, we keep at it because, as parents, we are on a mission, not a popularity contest. And so, I kept at my note writing—on and off. I admit that over the years, I've wondered if it made a difference. *I* loved getting notes in my lunch. I saved them. *My* customer? Not so much. And well, because my experience is obviously the best (and only) measure of reality, because she did not react in kind, I figured they just weren't that important. Well, clearly, I was wrong.

Picture the after-school scene: I am once again removing a crumpled note, and so I remark, "Should I keep putting these in your lunch? I mean, they're still here. Maybe you don't want them?" If I could use a slo-mo effect in writing, I would. Like the gears of reality changing tempo, she looked up as if I'd suggested we cancel the summer. "No! I like them. I just need a way to save them." Huh.

I had assumed that there was a simple equation when it came to gratitude. If it were important, then it would be evident. Since the crumpled remains were left for me to deal with, I took that as Exhibit A in the gallery of unappreciated gestures. Maybe there were other assumptions I ought to rethink. How do I react when life according to my equation doesn't play out? I might be tempted to think that my efforts go unnoticed. I was ready to retire from note writing. Why bother? Futility is a miserable place to live. But what if we trust that our efforts *are* valued?

My daughter and I started a new system. A lunch box note bag has been assigned to these daily gestures of love. She is saving them. And I, in turn, am motivated to write them. All it takes is knowing that she is reading my words. I'm not there to see it; it's an honor system. I'm even having more fun with it, adding stickers, coming up with witty messages, because I am feeling heard. All that changed was my perception; my sense that what I have to offer matters.

It's one thing with a kid; it's another with G-d. When the outcomes we crave don't land in our lap, it's tempting to give up. Why bother? In a results-driven world, achievements seem like the only measure of value. But there is another way. It comes in the smile of a child, the just-enough-money for the bill, the surprise parking spot right in front of the store. Those are the ways Hashem says, "I love what you're doing. Don't stop. Keep talking to me. Keep praying. I may not operate on your terms. But I'm watching. I'm reading. I am treasuring every word you send My way, every whisper of your soul."

What my daughter reminded me was that there is more than one way to respond and react. I may have my way of seeing reality, equating cause and effect, but that's not the only way. If it's true with our kids, it is ever truer with G-d. We think things ought to play out a certain way, we make deals, expecting our requests to be granted in return. But there isn't one way for G-d to respond any more than there is a singular way to appreciate a lunch note—there are infinite ways we can be answered.

Those notes are my attempt to connect and express my love. The goal is not about the pen and paper; it's the relationship. And that's the Divine message hidden in a lunch box. That our work is to build a relationship with our Creator—to send our own loves notes and requests, all the while knowing, it's not the specific result we most need—it's the connection. I had almost given up on sending those written reminders, but I didn't—because I listened closely. We can listen closely to our lives, finding G-d's presence in the details. And then one day, when we look up from our busy minds and longing selves, we will hear a voice asking, "Did you pack Me a note?" And we will be able to say, "Yes."

Every morning I watch my neighbor leave for work.

I can pretty much set my watch by him. He starts out just about the time I am puttering around in the kitchen, making coffee and getting lunches in order. It's early. He walks in what looks like a calm rush. He carries only his iPad and, as he glances to wave goodbye to his child, he begins to read from it. It's a bit like a silent film unfolding through the window.

As he is on his way, I can see his young son lingering in the window. The pajama-clad boy presses his face up against the glass. My neighbor turns the corner north toward the subway and I am left to linger between my own morning routine and the still-unfolding reel across the way. Usually within minutes, a caregiver comes to coax the child away.

I get busy with my caffeine needs and think little of it. Until the next morning, when we all simply repeat the routine. I sometimes wonder what it's like from his side. Does he take note of my silhouette darting between sink, fridge, and coffee mug? If this were a silent film, would the director pan from the outside into my home as well? Perhaps there's even a silent-film-style soundtrack.

This week, we deviated from the script. All parties were at their posts. I entered the kitchen and glanced up to see my neighbor exit his door right on cue. But this time, instead of a quick wave-and-I've-got-to-go, he stopped. This is likely where the director decides to play with the camera angle or music.

Something was different this morning. He was in less of a rush. From where I stood I could not see the child in the window. But I could surmise his presence from my neighbor's miming. There he stood, waving at first. Then he began to sign: first pointing at his eye, then making a heart with his hands, and ending off with an emphatic finger pointing back. You get it. The well-known mime for "I love you." A huge smile spread across my neighbor's face. He repeated the miming, offered a wave, and set off around the corner as per the usual script. But something was still different. And it wasn't the neighbor or the child still bopping by the window.

*It was me.* Something about my side of the script was altered. Just when I thought I knew what to expect, the script changed. I guess silent films have a way of doing that.

There are no mistakes in this life. The Almighty sends the exact Director's Cut required by our soul. It was clear to me that in the change of routine, in my witnessing this event, I had found a gem.

Routines can lull us into thinking nothing will change—they put us on autopilot where we stop paying attention and miss what *is* changing. But that morning the routine shifted, and I saw something new: a silent love affair playing out across the street. Sometimes the greatest expressions of affection come without words.

This father was not confined to syllables. His gestures transcended the walls of our houses, the distance between us, and certainly the impending separation between him and his child. In that moment, there was crystal-clear clarity: "You are mine. I love you. Even when I leave, even when you cannot hear me—I am here for you."

It was a gentle reminder to keep watching. I also find myself (sometimes still pajama clad) pressing my face up against the window of my life, wondering where my Father is. Maybe now I'll look a little harder, to see Him signing His love back at me.

*"Know Him in all your ways and He will direct your paths."*

*(Mishlei 3:6)*

It was nearing sunset when I decided to squeeze in a quick run. Time straddled two worlds: both day and night, dusk seemed to soften the edges of objects and reality. Coming up a hill, the light of the setting sun hit my eyes, causing me to squint.

Slightly out of breath, I made my way around a corner and up another incline, the last minutes of daylight slipping away. My focus was straight ahead with a single goal in mind—making it home with miles logged.

While absorbed in my own mental agenda, something caught my eye. At the side of the road stood a small figure—a little boy, no older than four years of age. As I drew closer, we locked eyes. He smiled and gave me a thumbs-up. I smiled back. Through this seemingly tiny gesture, it felt like he had whispered a belief in me. My stride lengthened. My efforts had been acknowledged. I was not alone. A moment of recognition seemed to shift reality, my tired feet became hero's footsteps on a meaningful trek. Dramatic? Maybe. The encouragement we all need? Absolutely.

How often are we traveling along the road of our life, destination in sight, when the light begins to fade? Our energy starts to drain, and we lose our sense of direction. It can be easy to lose hope of ever finding our way. We wait. We search. We long for clarity. We look for road signs that direct us: "Turn that way," "Commit to this guy," or, "It's going to be OK, honey." Despite our longing, the encouragement we crave rarely shows up that way.

Perhaps this is the point. It's when our clarity fades and the road hits an incline that we need to look closely in order to see the messengers standing at the side of the road. They are people and experiences that whisper, "You can do this!" and, "Keep going!" They are usually hidden in seemingly everyday encounters. Parking spots when we are rushed, a smile when we are lonely, and yes, a smile and thumbs-up from a four-year-old pedestrian. G-d unfailingly sends signs, but they require decoding. Our work is to notice them.

In his innocence, that boy will never know what he did for me on that late afternoon. He reminded me that embedded in the uphill moments of life, there are tiny cheerleaders waving for our attention.

If only every challenge could be reduced to a metaphor—neatly tied up in a story about a run, a child, and the setting sun. That would be too easy. Finding our way is not for the faint of heart. It requires gumption and commitment. Most of all, it requires the awareness that just when the light is leaving, just as our energy is sapping, that is when we need to look the hardest and listen the most deeply. We will hear quiet voices of encouragement, we will discover untapped reserves of courage. Finding the messages along our route strengthens our resolve and gives meaning to our struggles. It's when we persevere along the road and take a glance backward that we see the guideposts were there all along.

It takes resolve to stand like Romeo longing for Juliet at a balcony, calling out a friend's name. If you have never tried to get a someone's attention this way, I suggest trying it out…you'll discover a lot about yourself.

It started with my Shabbos afternoon plans—I would need to get into an apartment building with a buzzer system. This can present a problem for the Shabbos observant, i.e., there is no buzzing on Shabbos. No worries; guests were assured that someone would be waiting by the door at an appointed hour.

For those who might be fashionably late, we could simply walk around to the back of her building, station ourselves by the second floor balcony, and holler. This surely would get my gracious hostess's attention, and someone would be dispatched to let in the straggling guests.

Cue my tardy arrival, no one waiting at the door, so I went traipsing to the back. I situated myself under the second floor balcony and told myself, *Go for it!*

"Hellooooo!" No answer.

"I'm heee-rrrrrrre!" No response.

My heart began to race a little and my thoughts picked up speed. *What if she never hears me? Am I bothering the neighbors? Perhaps I won't get in at all?!* I let out one more call. It was useless. Of course, I could hear my own voice and so could anyone walking by. But the one person I most wanted to hear me was simply not tuned in. This got me wondering: Perhaps, in another way, *I* was the person who really needed to tune in and listen up.

Shouting out to the world—that is to say, looking for attention or understanding—can have us screaming and waving our arms in ridiculous directions. It's not always with our words and voices that we vie for attention. The way we speak, the choices we make, and the careers we choose are all bids to be seen; we long to be recognized for who we are and what we might become. Sometimes these bids seem to go unnoticed, leaving us deeply frustrated.

Standing beneath that balcony, sweat forming around my temples, discouraging thoughts swam through my head. *Would she ever hear me?* I was about to give up—until I realized, it wasn't her attention I needed most, it was my own. The greater message was my necessity to call out and listen deeply to my own voice.

Getting our own attention for long enough to check in and take our spiritual pulse can be an unsettling experience. Especially when we think we need to get someone else's attention. But it's the moments we stop waiting for someone else to say, "Yes, I hear you," that we call out most powerfully. It's there that we can listen to our own voices, understanding our deepest wants and desires. With this clarity, we can better express our needs in relationships and more clearly call out to Hashem.

The irony is that we need to listen to ourselves before we can ask another to hear us. The gift is that in better articulating our desires, we deepen our relationship with both ourselves and G-d, the ultimate Provider.

I circled to the side of the building and asked the Almighty to find another way to get me inside. Indeed, two people were leaving just as I reached the door. Slipping inside, I realized I had indeed been heard. Answers seem to have their own timing and paths of arrival. Our work is the job of asking—and then, listening carefully. When we do, we are better equipped to practice the art of truly calling out.

**"From the depths I called You Hashem."**

*(Tehillim 130:1)*

There is nothing like being alone to realize you really aren't. It's a bit like needing the darkness to notice the light.

I had the opportunity to visit one of our city's fine hospitals with a friend who was having surgery. Accompanying someone to a hospital is a bit like entering an alternate universe populated by busy staff, blue-gowned patients, and anxious families. Once in the inner sanctum of the building, there are no windows—at least not to the outside—only those looking in to check-in desks and post-op rooms. This experience, coupled with the stress of a medical procedure, has a way of warping time. Who knows if it's 3:00 AM or 3:00 PM? The day becomes measured by markers on the surgical route: registration, pre-op, post-op recovery, discharge nurse... Any of us who have spent time in a hospital know this feeling, where hours are marked by the change of nursing staff and days melt one into the other.

Having an anchor becomes crucial. We need some way of staying tethered to the outside world, a sense that we are more than this experience. This is where a designated "support person" comes in. It might be Mom or Dad, a close friend, or a child. It's the person who says, "I'm in this with you today." They remind the nurse when pain meds run low, they are a second set of ears when reports come in, but most important is their presence.

On this day, I saw a little Indian boy, no older than four, waiting to go in for surgery, accompanied by an entourage. As he bounded around the pre-op waiting area in his pediatric hospital gown (printed with trucks and all) his parents, grandparents, and uncle, (I think) watched in delight. We exchanged smiles as the boy played doctor, pretending to check their heartbeats.

So, when the admitting nurse kindly requested that "only Mom and Dad" accompany him to the next phase, my heart sank a little. They nodded, turned to each other conferring in Hindi, and then said good-bye to the rest of their crew. As I sat, new patients entered the room. Like a surgical train station, everyone gets their ticket and then waits. To my right sat a young woman. Alone. Two rows ahead, an older gentleman, likewise, unaccompanied. And I, in my busy imagination, began to wonder: *Why are they alone? Are they OK? Do they need something?*

Now here's the thing about a shared hospital space—sometimes boundaries melt away. Sometimes we are invited to share and connect in our parallel journeys. Other times, however, the boundaries don't melt at all. They stay strong. Necessary protectors of privacy. I recognized sitting in the pre-op room that day that this was not a "please come chat with me" moment. No one was inviting conversation between strangers in this waiting room. So I did all I knew how. I looked about until we casually made eye contact and offered a subtle smile. The older gentlemen offered one back. That was it. I soon left the waiting area, but carried with me a heavy heart for these lone patients.

At the end of the day, walking through the parking garage, now alone, a young woman crossed my path. She looked up and smiled. I smiled back. I might not have been a lone patient, but I likewise wanted someone with me. And then I got it. It's true, we are alone. Those patients might have someone waiting on the other side. They might not. But in the moment, when we feel this aloneness in the shared waiting room of life, we can make a choice to connect. It's the sense of our solitude that drives us to reach out. We need not run from this experience; it is an invitation to seek a relationship—with ourselves, each other, and ultimately with G-d.

When we feel our essential isolation, it's a chance to hear the Almighty's call: *You need not feel alone, come closer, look for Me.* When we realize that each of us is indeed on our own, the need to feel G-d's presence intensifies. To the degree to which we build a meaningful relationship with our Creator, we will never be alone. Searching for His presence in the details of our lives is the route to building this relationship.

And that's why there's nothing like being alone to see that you aren't—because those are the moments when we most powerfully seek

G-d's presence. It will show up in all different ways: the butterfly on your path, the song on the radio, and sometimes in a stranger's smile. Who knows? Maybe you are someone's smiling stranger today. Maybe you're the messenger of G-d's Presence.

"And how are you, sweetie?" she greets me most mornings.

Sharon, working in the cafeteria. Gray hair pulled back in a net, she smiles and calls me "love." There's a special lilt to her Newfoundland accent, as if she might break out into a limerick at any moment. "There you go, darlin'" she smiles, as if we have a little secret.

Our conversations range from the weather to her work schedule (starts early, ends early). One time, as I lingered getting my coffee, I inquired about her kids. She spoke of them in the wistful tone of someone who is no longer in the thick of child rearing. She didn't miss a beat as we chatted, never dropping her smile or pausing from her work. I admire Sharon. There is a steadiness to her. An even sense of being. I delight in her presence. I always walk away feeling like I've had a peek at some buried treasure. I've spent a few minutes feeling loved, just for showing up. I'm sure I'm not the only one. It's just her way. We all feel a bit like her favorite.

There are no airs about Sharon. She is not an act or a self-improvement project. It's just the way "folk ought to be," she would explain. It's her seeming simplicity that I love. I might be in the middle of the biggest thought storm, and there she will be, calm and still like a lighthouse.

As I pondered why it is that I love Sharon, the first thing that came to mind was her reliability. I can count on her greeting. I can expect her response. Her smile doesn't waver. Regardless of the weather, my internal angst or the rush I am in, her kindness doesn't change. And that is what I crave. Who doesn't? Whether it's uncertainty on the world stage or in your bank account, we all live with a fluctuating tolerance for the unknown.

Don't you wish someone could just put their hand on your shoulder and say, "Honey, I've got this." Maybe that's the secret smile Sharon gives me. It's telling me, "Sweetheart, I can't guarantee much beyond this moment, but I'm here now." Something about her way of conveying that allows me to show up with the same constancy and kindness, if even just for a moment.

You may have your own "Sharon." Maybe it's a friend, a doctor, or a sister. They are our angels of stability. Their kindness may be sharing a daily joke or a weekly smile. Their magic is not just that they're sweet sometimes (much as I love being called "sweetie"), it's their constant goodness. I look forward to my coffee pick up, not only for its caffeine supply, but because I get fifty seconds of love. And that is downright Divine.

Our Sharons are G-d's way of telling us, "I am constantly here for you." True, the world will do its up-and-down thing. We can't ever know what's around the corner. The Sharons of the world are reminders that even on our worst days, when we act out and throw adult tantrums, Hashem's love never waivers.

I watched her help a young man find the skim milk this morning. He was confused by the containers. With that trademark lilt in her voice, she pointed at the label, "There it is, darlin'." Not rocket science. But steady and kind. And sometimes, that's what we need most. To feel that there is a Rock, there is someone we can depend on. Who knows? Maybe *you* are somebody's Sharon, someone's reminder that Hashem is there. You don't need to make grand gestures or say much—you just need to be a steady voice of love, that smile each morning and a listening ear. As for my Sharon—I love it when she calls me "sweetie."

It's hard not to survey the contents of someone else's suitcase when it is wide open right in front of you. It was a Saturday night, and a group of excited nine-year-olds gathered in my home for a sleepover. I was making their beds when I caught sight of a mini overnight suitcase with the usual staples: socks, pajamas, change of clothes…and several stuffed animals. In fact, at least half the suitcase was taken up by well-loved furry friends. How sweet. How delightful to be at a stage of life where the absolute essential is a teddy bear. Can you imagine using half your luggage real estate for something so wholly impractical?

Nestled between these furry creatures and socks I noticed a deeper truth: what we pack into our proverbial luggage *ought* to be sources of comfort. Perhaps this young lady knew a secret I had forgotten: the things we require most in the nighttime of our lives are not always what we think. Just when we are sure that we have figured out what we need to weather the storm, life sends us a new forecast. Planned for rain? Here's the sun. Packed for snow? Surprise—it's unseasonably warm! Those are the moments when we need to recalibrate—not just our direction, but what we think will help get us on the way.

Teddy was smiling at me from his suitcase. I offered him a smile back. In that moment it was like winking, acknowledging Hashem-sized messages delivered in baggage: sometimes comfort and connection *are* the most essential items on our packing list. Teddy would be the young lady's source of comfort—where was mine?

There is no telling what the next moment or tomorrow may bring. We hope. We plan. We build. But the only certainty with which we can arm ourselves is a deep knowing that we are not alone. Like that teddy nestled in the suitcase, G-d is with us each step of the way. The more we pack this knowledge with us, the more we remind ourselves of this truth, the more it will fill the contents of our soul-sized baggage.

The degree to which we develop a meaningful relationship with Hashem is the degree to which we will never be alone. Whatever happens, we will be comforted in the presence of a loving Creator. We will be sent on far-off journeys, unexpected layovers, and overnight adventures. It's on those journeys that we refine and define who we are; it is through this process that we become ourselves.

At each turn we are called to decide: What will we carry? I'm thinking it's time I started taking packing tips from the under-ten set: prioritizing not just the "seemingly essential" items, but those soft reminders of G-d's love, security, and hope.

*"I will bless you, and I will make your name great, and you will be a blessing."*

*(Bereishis 12:2)*

Remember when the only kind of mail you got came through a slot in your door or a box attached to your house?

As a child, it was exciting because mail meant birthday party invitations, pen pal letters, and fun catalogs. I recall the feeling of anticipation—coming home and wondering if there was something for me. Long gone are those days. Most of my mail now consists of bills and electronic statements.

Still, I sometimes catch a sense of childish wonder as I enter my home. What might be there for me today? So, you can imagine my excitement when I arrived home to a find a package waiting for me. It was smallish and white with bubble wrap padding and my name and address handwritten. I racked my brain...Had I ordered something online and forgotten? No. Was I expecting something? Definitely not. What could it be?

I opened it, discovering a wrapped, broken shard of a plate. Strange. There was a card from a friend, one who now lives far away. In the card, she explained that this ceramic offering was from the plate broken at her *tena'im*, a contractual part of her wedding ceremony. Tradition suggests that this can bring blessing—increasing the flow of G-d's abundance as it manifests in this world. When we give a blessing, we are saying that we want to be part of that flow, that we want to make ourselves a conduit for G-d's goodness. This surprise package was her way of sending some of this energy my way.

She wrote that she'd intended to send it since her wedding, some years ago. She hadn't managed to get it to me, but had been holding onto it, wanting to send it...until now.

I was touched. Humbled. But perhaps most of all, I was inspired. Her gesture was so thoughtful, and what struck me most was her willingness to send that package to share the blessing, even so long after the initial thought of doing so. She has marked her wedding anniversary several times. She has become a mother, changed jobs, packed up homes, and moved countries, and all the while she carried this piece of plate and the gift of her intent—to share the blessings she has received.

How often have I thought, *I should give so-and-so a call*, and not followed through? Or wanted to give my condolences, share a thought, or reach out to someone? Then the moment passes, time lapses, and I fall into the trap of believing, *It's too late. I can't do that anymore. It might be awkward. I've missed the boat.* And so, I let it go. I'm sure I'm not alone in this experience.

What I saw in that package was a perfectly wrapped, came-right-through-the-door-slot piece of old-fashioned mail with a message expressly for me: It is never too late to give a blessing. The constant call of each moment is to recognize the Almighty's hand in our lives. When we catch a glimpse of G-d's goodness, it's our responsibility to share that awareness, asking ourselves: *How can I pay it forward? What is my unique way of blessing in this moment of my life?*

The package was an invitation of sorts to follow through on the gestures we think we've lost the chance to realize. It is never too late to show up. We can grab the opportunity—now—to pick up the phone. We can start smiling at the neighbors we never talk to. We can tell an acquaintance that we are sorry for their loss or ask a friend if she needs help—even if the moment of apparent need has passed. You'll be surprised by how kindness connects and how grateful people are when we share.

Blessings do not come with a best-before date. They are here for the taking and giving. I'm holding onto that piece of plate from my friend's *tena'im*. It's a reminder that in our broken world, we can be a part of the healing. We can be a blessing.

## ——————— YOUR TURN: GUIDE QUESTIONS ———————

- Do you speak to G-d in your own words? Set aside time each day to talk to G-d. Can you bring your genuine self to this most important relationship?
- What are you grateful for in your life? Make it a daily practice to thank and praise G-d for the gifts you have and ask for help in at least one area of your life.
- What is a small kindness you have experienced this week? Can you see how G-d is communicating His love to you through this experience?
- What is a blessing in your life? How can you pay it forward? What is one way you can share the gifts Hashem has given you with another?
- What helps you feel G-d's closeness? Can you think of a time you felt G-d's presence in your life? What can you build into your daily schedule to tap into this feeling?

# CHAPTER 7

# Hope

"I have truly hoped in Hashem, and He inclined
toward me."
*(Tehillim 40:2)*

After a mild winter, the fluffy white stuff arrived way past the point when spring "should have" been here. Weather reporters came out with statements that almost had you thinking that one of the ten plagues had hit. It was as if the cold precipitation was on par with locusts hitting an unsuspecting metropolis.

As you may know, I am not a lover of winter. I feel anxious at the very mention of winter boots. I envy those who ski, skate, and snowshoe, and those who get excited at the thought of subzero temperatures, active days, and cozy winter evenings. I am not made of such stuff. However, an April snowfall? *That* I can get into. Given my delight with the spring snow, I was pretty shocked when a friend, one of those "winter is awesome" sportspeople, plopped herself down next to me and declared, "I hate this snow!" She went on to describe her feeling that this was "downright weather chutzpah." She was not impressed.

If you are nodding your head in agreement, let me explain my side of things. Like I said, I am no cheerleader for cold weather. But when it snows in the spring, I am calm because I know it won't last for long. With the promise of summer sunshine just around the corner, I feel I can make it through a storm or two. It's when the winter seems eternal that I become discouraged.

Having shared this perspective with my friend, she explained that while my thoughts were "appreciated" (you can imagine just how appreciated they were...) she was done with winter, exclaiming, "If it can snow in April, who knows what May might bring?"

Then I got it.

We weren't simply talking about the weather; we were talking about hope and trust that things can change and get better. My friend was tired of winter, of working hard to make it through the cold, and in her fatigue, she was doubting the arrival of spring. That, I understood. I may feel calm in the face of April snow, but I know the kind of thinking that has us all wondering if we can keep hoping in the face of another disappointment. When we think that this time, this chance, or this relationship will be the one that works out and it doesn't, we are left with our hope-o-meter running low.

A friend can point out the weather trends, the reasons to trust that spring or an easier day will indeed arrive. But when we are flooded by hopeless thinking, it's hard to see past this moment.

Living low on hope isn't just painful—it's dangerous. We become untethered, disconnected from our purpose and our sense that change is possible. If gravity keeps our feet on the earth, hope allows us to climb heavenward. It's not about empty assurances or guarantees that everything will be "just fine," but the belief that a future different from the one we are imagining is possible, and that we can be part of making it so. It's a radical way to live—to have faith in a better future, to believe that we can heal pain and change lives. It can be tiring to hold onto this belief, particularly in a world that suggests yesterday is the best predictor of tomorrow. History may be filled with darkness and difficulty, but time and again we have risen when it seemed impossible, and seen the season change when it felt like it never would. Our mission is to continually recommit to hope.

You may not be suffering from hope fatigue, but I can guarantee that there is someone in your orbit running low on the belief that it's going to get better. We all need help re-believing in ourselves and the world. When we live with even a small spark of hope, the most wintery days become bearable.

I think I may even advocate for snow every spring. To be visited by a surprise weather system and then watch as warmth creeps around the corner is a real-time lesson in hope. When we look at the seasons, our days and our lives, knowing that a few unexpected storms are part of our soul journey, then we can grow hope in the most arid-seeming soil. It doesn't take much: a daily declaration that we believe in change, a look at our rich history of resilience, a mantra of optimism. As for this April, I'm ready for the snow to melt.

I almost lost something very important. Let me backtrack. A friend had lent me book, a decidedly risky move. This might not qualify as daredevil behavior for everyone, but I start worrying about returning an item the moment I borrow it. My high school librarian can vouch for my generous support of the school's book collection through late fees. I imagine that some of you can relate.

Still, I believe in change. So, when a hard-to-come-by book was offered on loan, I cautiously accepted. You know where this is going. At first, I read it, putting its contents to good use. Then it lingered on my dresser. I started to tell myself, *You ought to return it.* I mentioned my intention to the lender. She reassured that I need not rush. Fabulous, permission to procrastinate. And so, weeks passed, I noted the book, felt some fleeting anxiety over its return, and let it blend in with the scenery. Weeks became months and the need to return got bumped to the bottom of my to-do list. Until I received a message asking if she could have it back. Sure. No problem. I pulled the book off the shelf, placed it in my car, and made a point of swinging by her home. All of this would make for a very boring screenplay, if it weren't for the plot twist ahead.

I knocked on the door (cue close-up camera lens to add an air of mystery). She answered (cue music). I gave her the book.

I had done it! Phew.

She looked at the book, smiled, and pointed out that *this was not her book.* Similar binding, same author. Not hers. That's when panic mode began, and the sneaky suspicion that I had no clue where her book was. I took the book back, reassured her I'd return with the correct item, and made my way home. And so, the search began. Lives might not have been at stake, but this felt like a near-fatal mistake. I was flooded with shame, berating myself for "being so irresponsible" and "messing this up." In my anxious state, finding that book felt like the only way to restore my sense of self. I had planned this another way. Yet, here I was, again. I had missed the mark. I was discouraged. It was supposed to be different this time, *I* was going to be different. And then I wasn't. Sigh. It was a self-deprecation party in my head.

These sorts of thoughts are not reserved for book-borrowing blunders: we set a goal, we plan to change, and then we don't. We fall into old patterns, we lose momentum, and then we lose hope. We get dragged into thinking that we "can't" or "won't" become who we want to be. We give up on dreams, we give up on ourselves. I was getting close to this feeling, but I wasn't quite ready to give up on finding the book.

I looked all over. I remembered its perch on my dresser—no longer there. I scanned my shelves—not in sight. I began to feel a little queasy. So obviously, the rational thing to do was to panic and begin madly messaging her: a string of apologies, distraught-faced emojis, *Where can I possibly find a replacement?* and *Is it possible I already returned it?* She agreed the latter might be the case. I continued searching and text panicking. Amid this fury, book-lending friend replied: *Cool your jets. It's OK.*

May we all be blessed with friends who can tell us lovingly when we need to simmer down. I took her direction. And in my state of relative calm I "happened" to see the book, high up on my bookshelf. It had been there all along.

Finding answers rarely happens in a fit of anxiety. The ironic thing about a frantic search is that our fear is blinding—it clouds our judgment and narrows our view of reality. We become so focused on the problem, real or imagined, that we can't see the remaining possibilities. We lose sight of our capacities and resources. Calming down opens up our blind spot. Taking a deep breath, a long walk, or a moment to reset helps us see ourselves and our lives more broadly—we can once again problem solve and explore new options. What seemed give-up-worthy in a state of panic becomes workable from a place of calm. Fearful thoughts impose self-limiting realities. We believe we can't, so we don't. Self-doubt is the enemy of change; it keeps us stuck where we most need to grow. We worry that we're incapable, so we dare not try. If fear and doubt disconnect us from our vitality, calm can reconnect us to our inner strength. The challenge is to cultivate our personal route back to that inner quiet.

The book had been on the shelf the entire time. The only thing I lost was a sense of myself, the feeling that I was the kind of person who could be trusted to borrow and return. Fear had me doubting myself and my capacity to change; quieting that fear helped me see what had been there all along. I'm not sure I'll be borrowing a book anytime soon, but I will be calling upon the "cool your jets" mantra when I start to panic.

**"Jealousy is the rot of the bones."**

*(Mishlei 14:30)*

A phone was ringing, and it wasn't mine. All I could do was smile.

Somewhere inside a locker, a familiar ringtone was going off and there was nothing I could, or should, have done about it. I loved that. It was the same relief that washes over me in the middle of a class or meeting when someone has forgotten to turn off their phone ringer. There is the momentary concern of, *Is it mine?* followed by a flood of relief. This one's not on me. So there that phone was ringing, and there I was, with nothing to do about it. A bliss born of clarity.

Let's imagine an alternative. I walk by the locker and hear the sound of the ringer. Even though my phone is at my side, something inside of me whispers, *I love that ringtone!* So instead of moving on, I linger just listening to the digital ditty. As I stand there, I get more and more excited, lusting after that phone. I start scheming: *How can I open the locker? Maybe I can break in? I really should...I owe it to that phone to liberate it.* Honestly, if its owner deserved it, she'd take better care of it—she'd have it with her. With a mounting sense of purpose, I forget that I have my own phone and have only one desire in my heart—finding a way to make the locker-oppressed phone my own.

Let's rewind this scenario to my moment of real-life relief. Why was I calmed when I realized that it wasn't my ringtone? Clarity. I have my own phone. That was someone else's. Beginning, middle, and end of story. So, what makes phone-ring envy any more bizarre than looking at someone else's house and thinking, *I'd appreciate it more if I lived there*, or scrolling through images of happy families/career successes/ fun vacations, and thinking, *Why not me?* Hidden in the question is the feeling that it ought to be me. Ringtones might have us reacting somewhere between irritated and relieved, but life, and sharing this planet with a host of other humans, is much more challenging.

We come into this world with a unique soul and circumstances that are individually prescribed by the Almighty. Our strengths and weaknesses, our families and our struggles, are gifted by G-d. What we do in those circumstances is up to us. Our choice lies in how we respond to reality, who we become through the context of our life.

The nice thing about ringtones these days is that they can be changed or customized. Perhaps Hashem also has some trademarked ringtones, ways that He tries to communicate to us. Our challenge is to listen for the sound of our own lives, noticing the details that make up our unique universe.

In my imagined cell phone scenario when I became so fixated on another phone, I completely forgot my own. Desire has a way of blinding us to what we already have. When we long for someone else's reality, we reject the opportunity to be uniquely us. If I'm busy lusting after your life, I forfeit the chance to build my own world. Envy is described in *Mishlei* as, "The rot of the bones," because it is the rot of the self. There is only one version of you and one version of me. There is only one point in time when this soul will collide with this moment. When we get busy listening in to other people's calls, missions, and lives, we miss our own.

I walked away from that locker with a smile on my face. It was an easy reminder to stay focused on what is mine and keep my ears open for the calls that *do* come, directed at *my* soul. Next time you hear a phone ring, maybe you'll smile too, thinking of that poor locker-bound phone. Unless of course, it is your phone ringing. In that case, you might just want to answer it.

As a lover of words, thought, and stories, it was the quotes that caught my attention on my visit to an art gallery. The curator had placed selected passages from the artist along the walls to accompany the exhibit. Yes, the artwork was beautiful...rich...interesting...but I was equally drawn to watching fellow patrons and pondering the artist's words posted by the works. These reflections on the artistic process were a small window into the world behind the paintbrush. One sentence in particular gave me chills. It read: *Every artist should travel to the south, so he can wipe clean his palette.*

Ah, to have our palette wiped clean. Start fresh. Reboot. To travel south. Wrapped up in the promise of travel is often the hope that the internal landscape might likewise shift, and the palette with which we paint our lives will brighten. While I'm no visual artist, the metaphor called to me and had me wondering: How can we rework our reality? Does it require a geographical cure? Or might there be the possibility for a fresh palette here and now?

Tired of the daily grind, it can feel like we need an overhaul. Moments when the script of "get up, get out, get home, repeat" becomes a monotone paint set are when we most crave that fresh start. It may feel like we need a major life overhaul, but small adjustments can be the most powerful way to cultivate a fresh perspective; it is less about changing our circumstances and more about changing ourselves.

The work of transformation begins with the everyday, breathing new life into our routines so that we become more curious and open. For example: taking a new route on our commute, savoring our morning coffee, or pausing to look and really listen when we usually rush. Finding fresh eyes and discovering more brilliant colors on the palette of life may be the most essential way we "travel south." With even the smallest tweaks in how we encounter the world, we change ourselves. Simple pleasures delight, wonder finds its way back into our days, and once-closed doors become possibilities. We can look at the canvas of our lives and see new colors, discovering that the fresh start we craved was there all along.

Words, quotes, and phrases come to inspire, but also to guide our thoughts toward truth. Becoming more aware that the One who presses the refresh button is doing so on a daily basis, creates an opening for our process to unfold. From this stance, we can keep our eyes peeled for the messages encoded in our everyday experiences.

When an artist longs for her palette to be "wiped clean" it is because she understands that there will then be room for fresh paints, new colors, and deeper expressions. When we see that our lives are likewise continually regenerating, then wherever we are, however much or little we travel, we can find the energy we need, and the possibility of a fresh start.

*"Then our mouth will be filled with laughter and our tongue will be glad with song."*

*(Tehillim 126:2)*

One of my favorite sources of inspiration these days comes from pictures of old ladies sitting on a park bench laughing together. This sort of image might appear with a thoughtful quote, a tongue-in-cheek comment, or a guideline to getting through life. Sometimes these laughing ladies appear on birthday cards, funny posters, and my news feed. Each time, I am drawn to a secret they seem to know, a place they appear to have reached.

I acknowledge that these are manufactured images. However, there is a whiff of reality that I am catching, a scent of truth that draws me in. These women seem to have lived long enough, played out enough of the story, to have a certain kind of "knowing," a letting go, a living more deeply. They have seen enough to know that what feels so "urgent" rarely proves important in the long run. Life experience has taught them that hidden in each challenge is something good, or at least a moment of shared laughter.

At times we smile and our hearts are still heavy. We join in the conversation, but our minds are traveling in a thousand directions. We are physically present, and emotionally absent. The ladies in these images appear to be present with their whole selves, laugh lines, eye creases and all. They are not only sharing something with each other...they are sharing something with us. They are letting us in on a secret earned over years of living—one day we will look back and see our struggles were leading us to joy.

Given that few of us are likely headed for modeling for one of these beautifully photoshopped inspiration-grams (pun intended), what piece of this puzzle is ours? The ability to find true laughter. Spiritual laughter is the expression of our soul in a moment when everything reverses: what looked like darkness is revealed as light. We laugh at a joke because of its unexpected turn. We laugh with our souls when we experience an unexpected turn, when what seemed like the end becomes a beginning, when what looked like darkness is revealed as the very source of light. It might be the moment we realize that the letter that told us "bad news" about health, school, or a job—was actually a love note from G-d, pointing us to an even better route. Those are the times we are let into the old-lady-kinda-laughter. We don't need to wait for old age to catch a glimpse of the truth, why not look for it now?

Each day we are alive is a vote of confidence from G-d—a sort of ratifying statement: "I believe in you, kid. You're worth sustaining 'cuz you've got a job to do and you're growing to accomplish it!" G-d believes in us; we also need to believe in ourselves. When we live with this trust, we are let in on the secret these lovely ladies seem to know.

The secret, the key to living with this sort of connected sense of abandon, is trusting that each challenge is an opportunity in disguise. Just as surely as we'll gain wrinkles and gray hair, we can gather wisdom and perspective. In retrospect, all the stuff that felt so hard or important will be revealed as part of a bigger plan. The small stuff we sweat rarely proves important in the end. And when it's the big stuff, real middle-of-the-night heartache, we can also hold onto that secret knowing that one day it will make sense and we will find joy in finally understanding.

True spiritual laughter is an expression of redemption. It's the realization that all along we were traveling toward wholeness, joy, and connection. The darkness was merely an illusion. And then, no matter our age or photo readiness, we can be just like those laughing old ladies...because we've been let in on one of life's great secrets.

*"Tracht gut, vet zein gut—Think good and it will be good."*
*(Yiddish Proverb)*

I really don't want to change my password...again.

I forget passwords. I make up new iterations (plus or minus the capital) and then I file them away with all the other "important information" in my mind. The problem is, it all starts to blend together. So, when my computer at work prompted me to update my password (as it does every three months), I was less than enthused. I could feel my resistance bubbling up. Weren't we all doing just fine with things as they were?

Well, clearly not. Or not according to the data security titans. I had no choice: create a new, ninety-day-passkey reality. I would have to type this over and over. Whatever word I chose would be on daily repeat mode.

I am no stranger to repetition, particularly in the land of thoughts. I wish my go-to thinking was full of hope and trust. Some days it is. But in the darker corners of my mind, I can be flooded by fear and doubt.

We all have our default script, the one that chants "I can't," "Why now?" or some version of an internal groan. Maybe yours is fancier, but the bottom line remains—we all fall prey to negative thinking. And once we start, it's hard to stop those mantras. Getting unstuck is not easily done. So, when it came to choosing a new password, I wondered if I could become a little more deliberate about what thought (or word) I would have looping on my mental airwaves.

I recall learning about the birth of subliminal messaging. Picture the scene, a 1957 movie theater. Unsuspecting viewers watched as "Eat Popcorn" and "Drink Coca-Cola" flashed across the screen. Allegedly the messages were too short for the viewer to be aware of, but long enough for the subconscious to pick them up. The field of marketing psychology and subliminal messaging has grown in recent years, highlighting that what we see and read will shape how we think and who we are. Words and images will become fodder for our internal tape.

Which brings me back to my password challenge. Sitting there, trying to dream up (yet another) word, I wondered if I might choose something meaningful. A statement I'd actually like to repeat over and over. And that's just what I did. I chose a reminder of how I want to see the world and who I might become.

I'm not giving away my password here. But suffice to say, each time I logged in during that ninety-day reality, I paused and remembered a simple, hopeful truth. It's a small step. Narrow thinking and less-than-cheerful feelings still find their way into the mix. But every time I typed those words, each moment I focused in that direction, I inched closer to a hopeful perspective.

We cannot banish all of our dark thoughts, nor can we think only good all the time. What we can do is make it a daily practice to bring our attention toward all that *is* good. When we express gratitude, count our blessings, and notice simple pleasures, we actually wire our minds to be more positive. Through repetition, we create internal pathways toward greater joy and hope. When we feel this way, we are more open and able to connect and grow.

So now, every time I'm prompted to change my password, I smile instead of sighing, knowing it's another chance to practice where I want to focus.

Maybe it's time to change your password?

————————— YOUR TURN: GUIDE QUESTIONS —————————

- What helps calm you? Experiment with setting aside five minutes a day to focus on your breathing and settle your mind.
- Scan your day for three good things that happened. Try this every day for a week. What do you notice? Do you naturally start "shopping" for more of the positive?
- What is an experience you had that looked bad but ultimately was for your benefit? Can you look at a current struggle and trust that it will likewise be for your ultimate good?
- We can train our minds to think more hopefully and focus in the direction we desire. Choose a mantra for a week—write it somewhere you will see it, program a reminder, or make it your password. Every time you say this mantra, you are wiring your mind to be more hopeful and connected.

# CHAPTER 8
# Connection

"As in water face reflects face, so the heart of man
reflects man."
(*Mishlei* 27:19)

*"Words are limited. Words, no matter how perfectly chosen and
eloquent, are fragments of meaning. They are the bits and pieces which
communication struggles to construct. If you are sensitive, you will
know that the deepest experiences are the most difficult to express."*
(Akiva Tatz)[5]

'm a big fan of emojis. Yes, those little characters and icons—hearts
and blushing smiley faces that pepper texts and emails. Like a dash of
colored sprinkles on a plain vanilla ice cream, they add some pizzazz
and playfulness to my written communiqués.

In the hustle-bustle of the everyday, actually talking to each other or
even making eye contact is a dying art form. How many times do you
walk into a room and everyone is staring down at an electronic device?
How often do you have a conversation while you're both looking at your
phones? In an increasingly fast-paced and automated world, emojis are
like a wink, a way of expressing, "Hey! I'm here and I see you." A picture
is worth a thousand words. Perhaps an emoji is worth fewer, but it is an
unmistakable "seize the graphic moment" in my day. I love it.

As I was discussing this pleasure with a friend, she quipped, "Emojis

---

5    *The Thinking Jewish Teenager's Guide to Life* (Southfield: Targum Press Inc., 1999).

show up as black boxes on my phone." This was on the heels of my receiving a text from another friend, explaining that my message to her was showing up with, "Eight empty squares"—completely emoji-less. *Lost in translation.* And so, I did the only thing I knew how—I spelled it out for her: *heart, heart, heart.*

In trying to express the unreadable message, I started to wonder about all the empty black boxes that flash across the screen of my life: *What am I losing in the translation?* What are all the ways I am missing the point, assuming I understand what someone else means but not really hearing what they are saying?

I had once approached a mentor, looking for the answer to a student's question. I posed the question and then waited for his wisdom to fill in the missing information. He paused, "What do you think she was *really* asking?" I restated the question. That wasn't what he was looking for. "Listen to what is beneath the surface; what is she really bothered by? Is she asking for more data here, or is she stating a need to better understand the world and how it works?" I paused again and searched in the spaces between her words. And then I heard her real question. She didn't want to know more facts; she wanted me to hear what was troubling her. What she meant was not what she had explicitly stated. It requires artful listening to really hear one another. It takes work to communicate and unlock the meaning behind each other's words.

When living in a "plain font" world where we take things at face value, it's easy to miss the deeper layers and nuances of communication. Can you imagine someone telling you that Times New Roman is the only typeset available? Or that emojis will be completely abolished? It sounds absurd, but that's what we do when it comes to talking. We assume that we mean the same thing because we use the same words. We become frustrated when people don't "get us"—but are we doing the work to "get them?"

I love emojis because they add something beyond language to the conversation. They fill in some gaps where tone and body language usually stand. We can be playful with them. We can be emotional. Yet texting is still a poor substitute for actual human connection. When we are more comfortable using emojis than we are giving a real-time smile or hug, we miss out on so much of our potential.

As my friend pointed out, sometimes emojis fall short, and we need to do the extra work of translating so that the other person can really hear our message. This means tuning in to *their* experience, tailoring our tone, and working to finding the right words for *each person*. We likewise need to be the careful listeners, attuning ourselves to the nuances of speech and expression.

If those smiley faces and thumbs-up signs can teach us something, it's to listen more deeply and express ourselves more fully. We need to tell the people we love, "I'm proud of you," offer a stranger a smile, or look a suffering friend in the eye so that she sees we are with her in her pain. Don't let anyone fool you into thinking this is a plain-font world. Language is a Divine gift for us to use. When we work at it, we can express sublime concepts and deep love through our words. And when what we have to say is beyond language, our faces and bodies can serve as powerful tools of communication. Some of the deepest emotions are the hardest to express. That is why real soul connection, when we feel truly seen and heard by another, is experienced in the space beyond finite language. It is what we all crave. It is one of life's deepest pleasures.

I remain a fan of emojis, but I will never look at them with quite the same eyes. They lost their simple meaning that day. They became a reminder of how we can all listen up and start really hearing each other.

I am always shopping around for inspiration and insight. So, it's not too surprising that when I was actually shopping, I stumbled upon a life lesson. I first saw it as I was waiting in line to pay. By the cash register. A display of perfume bottles. In a world where all is eye candy, the packaging was sleek and modern. Anyone in branding and marketing will tell you that you have about three seconds to win over the customer. After that, you've lost your window. It should grab you on the spot. Product names are chosen to seduce, as was the name on that perfume package: Gossip.

I paused to reread. Maybe I'm naive, but it caught me by surprise. I know enough to understand—what sells, what lures, what is valued. This wasn't a high-end product, but there it was calling out: *Gossip*.

No thank you.

Sometimes the items we choose *not* to buy speak more powerfully than those we take home. I remember working in retail and delighting in honestly telling customers my opinion. A woman would stand at the mirror in a less-than-fabulous outfit and turn to me. "What do you think?" I'd pause. "The truth? You can do better." A simple soul-defining moment. I could be honest, and she could walk out free of an unneeded item. That's how it is with some of the more tempting stuff in life. Gossip (and its namesake perfume) is one case in point.

I had no desire to buy that bottle. But I am tempted to say or listen to words better left unsaid.

The packaging is more alluring. Sharing a juicy bit of information does make us feel in the know. A catty comment will give momentary satisfaction. When we choose these fleeting pleasures, we are buying cheap perfume. It might look nice on the shelf, but once you get home, it's nothing but a second-rate pleasure.

I imagine the marketing team brainstorming names for this perfume. They have it down to three choices. They lean in, examining their customer retail patterns. And they vote: Gossip wins. What I doubt they realized is the genius in its label—it is the perfect description of its namesake. Both gossip and cheap perfumes spread and linger with their sickening odor. The first burst might be nice, but it doesn't take long to irritate or even repulse. And try as you might to remove it from your life, it will remain on the collar of your coat or along the handle of your purse. You never have as much control as you think you do. That marketing team captured a deep truth about both perfume and our words.

Talk may be cheap, but we all pay a high price when we lose respect for the power of our speech. Words are important because they are our tools of expression. Our mouths can be the vessel of connection, our speech the glue of relationships. We can likewise use this power to put each other down, divide and destroy. We don't set out with this intention any more than we plan to make poor purchases—but they have much in common: both impulse shopping and gossip are symptoms of self-distrust. We feel fundamentally insecure, imperfect in ourselves, and we try to fill that void. When we gossip, we buy into the illusion that by emphasizing another's faults we somehow prove our own superiority. The problem is that we can't fill an internal hole by poking holes at someone else.

Seeing those bottles marked "Gossip" made it clear that the world is selling a cheapened version of reality. We are flooded by messages that compromise us: our bodies, our minds, and yes, our speech. It was easy to walk away from the perfume display; it's much harder to find kind words or bite our tongue. We are familiar with quick fixes and easy ego boosts; we are yet to be experts in the fine art of speech. Choosing how and when we speak is the mastery of careful consumption. It's time we took on the challenge. Remember those women I'd advise against buying a less-than-great outfit in my retail days? They always walked out head up, with a smile. It was a confirmation of their worth, "Honey, you deserve better." We all do.

*"In a tantalizing paradox, the ability to make ourselves vulnerable is actually the biggest strength we have. It is through receiving that we increase the amount of love, abundance, and joy in our lives."*
(*Miriam Kosman*)[6]

Every time I attend a live performance, my faith in humanity is restored. The very fact that a mass of people is gathered in such a civilized manner to watch a group of individuals perform, and that all parties have agreed to engage in a cultural activity together, is hope inspiring.

So, it wasn't much of a stretch to listen as an opera-fan friend extolled the virtues of a particular performance. I'm no opera connoisseur, but I could relate to the marvel of the staging, the training, the agreement

---

6    *Circle, Arrow, Spiral* (Jerusalem: Nefesh Yehudi, 2014).

between audience and performers to show up and witness a story told in many notes—both literal and figurative.

At a musical I had recently attended, I delighted not just in the song, dance, and costumes. I also spent a good deal of time imagining behind the scenes: the planning, building, and directing. When I shared that I'd been picturing the musicians in the orchestra pit with a violinist friend, she had beamed and thanked me for supporting the arts.

Perhaps most remarkable is that theater going is more than supporting or witnessing: it is a transactional event. Through the very act of showing up, all parties agree to both give and receive in specific ways.

The audience-performer relationship is most palpable when the actors come out and bow. We cheer and clap, and then they motion in gratitude to the audience. The fourth wall melts away and they look right at us as if they are saying, "We need you, maybe even more than you need us. If you aren't here, there is no one to accept what we have to give." What they are expressing with a seemingly simple gesture of their arms is that there is an art to receiving. The simple act of watching the performers—sitting in the dark and taking in what they have to—requires an openness of eyes, heart, and mind. With a not-so-simple shift in self, we can cultivate the art of truly receiving.

While *taking* is an insatiable and ego-driven act, *receiving* is the art of accepting what the other longs to give. I *take* because I want. I *receive* because I desire a relationship with the giver. You may not want to eat the rock-hard cookie your kid has baked, but you accept it because you love the child and want to give them the gift of giving to you. The difference between taking and receiving is not about what we get, but how we go about obtaining it. I can take a chocolate bar simply because I crave its sweet pleasure, or I can receive it as a delicious gift.

Sitting down to see a play, watch an opera, or take in the music of a street busker requires an inner pause: you might have 101 errands to run, you may have just endured a personal World War III, but for that moment, you lay it all down to simply receive the performer. That's where the magic happens—in the very commitment to the relationship. I will watch, and you will show. I will be present with you. *I* will turn off and tune into to *you* and what you want to share.

We clap as a way of participating in the show, sometimes louder than others, to acknowledge not just skill and talent—but that we have a role to play in the exchange. We have an equally critical role to play in our relationships. Our loved ones bid for our support and attention, they invite us to witness their inner world, sharing hopes and worries. Do we listen? Do we show up as if we have front-row seats to the most exquisite performance? Or do we turn away, offering half attention or outright rejection to their bids for connection?

Our relationships will grow or dwindle depending on how we use these moments. The excited child who wants to tell you about his day is offering you a precious gift. The spouse who asks for affection is saying, "I need you to be with me." The friend who courageously tells you her never-shared past is begging for you to receive her story. Becoming someone who can really receive is a skill to practice every moment of our lives. And when we are alone, we can notice G-d as the ultimate Giver.

My violinist friend was grateful for my support of the arts. How different would life be if we started supporting each other with the same kind of enthusiasm? We are invited to a live performance each day. There's no curtain call or orchestra pit, but if you watch carefully, you will see the opportunities to turn toward the people in your life and receive what they long to give. When we do that, we become experts in the art of receiving, for *that* is truly worth applauding.

**"It is not your responsibility to finish the work [of perfecting the world], but you are not free to desist from it either."**

**(Pirkei Avos 2:16)**

It's good to live in a country where there is a waste disposal system. It's even better when the garbage actually gets picked up. Rewind to an early morning. A friend and I were standing on the curb when a garbage truck stopped along its route. From the side of the vehicle, a forklift-like mechanism reached out, hoisting a garbage bin up and over, emptying its contents and returning the bin to the curb. Engineering at its best.

The truck inched along to the next house, ready to repeat the task. Only this time, there was a glitch. Somewhere between forklift and hoist, the bin wiggled out of grip, landing on its side and leaving a trail of trash on the sidewalk. We watched as the truck inched to the next house.

It seemed that the garbage would remain behind along with the toppled bin. We were not impressed; it was downright disgusting. We wanted better for our neighborhood, city, and world. It might seem hyperbolic, but these little oversights seemed symptomatic of a greater abdication of responsibility. If bins are abandoned along the route, what else are we neglecting? We trailed off, lamenting the state of our planet and society. But, we cast our judgment too soon.

My friend and I watched as the driver got out of his truck, walked back to the scene of events, and began collecting all the strewn waste. Piece by piece he picked up its contents, carrying the bin back to his truck and then setting it straight on the curb. We marveled at this unexpected twist of fate. It would have been easy enough to drive off. He had a long route ahead.

We are no strangers to leaving a mess, to wanting to keep going without dealing with the chaos in our wake. Our messes might be a friend's hurt feelings, a needy child, or unfinished paperwork. It is tempting to walk away or turn a blind eye, which made the garbage man's efforts all the more appreciated. We couldn't bear silent witness—we thanked him and literally applauded his act. He was grateful to be noticed and we felt even better. A win for humanity.

The story could have stopped here, but it doesn't. As he drove off, my friend quickly took note of his truck number. She was going to call. I might have made it as far as jotting the number and then losing the info at the bottom of my purse. But my friend made it to the call. The nice thing about having friends who go above and beyond is the inspiration through association.

"I spoke to the supervisor and got connected to the driver. I told him how amazing what he did really was. He said that no one had ever called to show appreciation for his work." The driver thanked her for the call. I was impressed. I wondered how much more motivated I'd be if I got applause every time I quietly cleaned up a spill or turned back to do the right thing. He had ended the call by explaining that, "A person has to take pride in whatever it is that they do."

There is no job too big or too small, no moment too grand or too mundane, to bring forward our best self, the part of us that believes in our worth and the power of our actions. We get fooled into thinking that the tasks that make it to a résumé or win applause are the most important. The nitty-gritty work of taking care of this planet and each other is rarely glamorous and seldom makes the headlines. But it is what counts. It's how we show up to whatever moment or person is in our path that defines who we truly are and defines what we are to become. When we respond to the needs before us, we take responsibility for our world. No one else is standing in our place. Therefore, no one else is positioned to see the world through our eyes or is able to repair it with our unique capabilities. When we give in to the voice that says, "I can't" or, "Why bother?" we miss the point: it's not a matter of fixing everything at once; it's the practice of answering with action.

I doubt the driver enjoyed collecting that trash, but he understood it was his responsibility in that moment. It was worth taking pride in what he alone could accomplish. We too are challenged on a daily basis to pick up the pieces—sometimes we've made the mess, sometimes someone's left it for us. Those pieces are calling to us, begging us to take pride, one task at a time. And when we do take responsibility, when we circle back to the mess, there may not be anyone watching or willing to go the extra mile and make a call of appreciation. That's when we need to call out to ourselves, *You showed up! Great job! There was a lot to deal with, and you kept going.* I'll never look at a garbage truck the same way. That man changed my world. As for the messiness of life, I'm trying to clean up, one bit at a time.

My favorite part of the concert was when it got quiet. Not completely silent, but when the volume came down. It had been a much-anticipated event: The Maccabeats live. I might have made out that I was only attending as chaperone for my daughter and her friend, but truthfully, I was equally excited. Having followed their *a cappella* success over the years, this was not our first show. I knew the drill, the parts where they talked between sets and how they got the crowd going.

But I forgot about one part—when they stop and acknowledge their sound crew and give a nod to the fact that, well, they aren't singing pure *a cappella*. Microphones, speakers, and audio tweakings that affect the carryover of their voices to our ears do count as performance-enhancing tools, even if at first glance they don't seem to be instruments.

And so, at a certain point the performers laid down their microphones and treated us to an unplugged performance. They moved closer. So did we. It was remarkable to watch as the very lively children stopped. Sat down. And really listened.

Leaning in, the voices became more audible. In the most no-frills performance there seemed to be the greatest power. It is a truth that kindergarten teachers around the world know: if you really want to get the class's attention, stop. Get quiet.

We forget this. We shout louder. We think that if our words or actions are bigger, more noticeable, they will have greater impact. We are mistaken. Business leaders know how to command a boardroom—it starts with a pause. People of power are not afraid of silence; they will linger in the space between question and answer to consider their words. They know the truth of a real *a cappella* performance: the less we say and the more considered and tempered our words, the more people listen.

How can we really be heard? Flashier, faster, and louder might get us quick notice, but is our message actually understood?

When we are frustrated or anxious, we tend to say more than necessary and become forceful. We worry that we won't be understood, so we do everything to make our point. Except we usually don't. We push people away instead of drawing them in. Our challenge in a world full of shouting is to reclaim the intimacy of hushed tones, to really listen to each other, daring to say less and pause more.

When we stop shouting and start speaking softly, we draw each other closer. This closeness creates a feeling of safety. When we feel safe, we can listen to each other. That's when the real conversation begins. It's when we don't need to compete or defend that we are able to communicate. This is the magic of turning down the volume.

Maybe next time we are tempted to get louder, we will stop and lay down our life-size microphones. We might just find the rest of the world, like the concert audience, leaning in to meet us.

***"You shall surely rebuke your neighbor."***

*(Vayikra 19:17)*

There are a range of possible reactions when we get lost—from total terror to utter delight. We each fall somewhere along that spectrum. We may even move back and forth depending on the day, the situation, and the destination. For those of us who recall the days of the seam-torn maps in the glove box, we know that getting lost is nothing like it used to be.

It wasn't so long ago when the only option was to pull over at the gas station and put yourself at the attendant's mercy, hoping they'd give good directions. Not anymore. Simply plug the destination into your handy mapping device, and a kind voice will guide you along the road. GPS, Waze, Google Maps—choose your fix—we've outsourced navigation, and with it our ability to independently find our way. Maybe not always, but to a large degree.

There are distinct advantages: Just when you think you're going the right way, your device will chime in to let you know, well, you're wrong. There were times you'd have to drive miles, finding yourself at the other side of town before there was any premonition of a wrong turn. It's not that we've solved the problem of getting lost—*we've changed the experience.*

I don't mind going a little off the expected route. I am partial to detours. They tend to lead to adventure and a good lesson. What I am sensitive to is the process of getting lost. If I'm going to find myself on the wrong road, I'd rather not have added stress or criticism. Like when you trip and someone blurts out, "Careful!" *after* you've taken a tumble.

Or when you've made a mess of your day and someone "helpfully" points out what you should have done differently. Thanks, but a little bit late for that advice. To be fair, I also offer this kind of patronizing wisdom. I know it's seldom useful. In fact, it probably makes things worse. Nothing like being told, "You're wrong!" to increase anxiety and drain self-confidence.

When the GPS chides, "Recalculating," I'm less than excited. It might just be me, but I have sensed her growing irritation as she recalculates over and over again. So, it was particularly pleasant when I noticed Waze's sing-song response to my wrong turn. No comment. Just a little notification and a new route suggested. I wouldn't be surprised if it started offering a latte as I continued driving. Seriously. It's worth driving the wrong way just to hear it. Wouldn't it be nice if we were as gentle with ourselves as Waze is?

The thing about being human is that wrong turns are part of the deal: comments we'd like to take back, choices that leave us wishing life had a rewind button, and times that we don't even see our errors. That's when our route needs recalculating. Whatever your reaction is to getting lost, you'll need to find a way to get back on course. Sometimes, even those of us with a well-calibrated internal compass simply can't get there alone. We need advice. We even need to listen to the after-the-fall commentary.

Criticism, delivered with compassion, is a greater act of love than letting it go. It's easier to look away or let behavior slide than to give a just-right rebuke. When we really care and believe in someone, we work at helping them grow. No teacher would be applauded for marking wrong answers correct. The skill is in knowing how to lovingly point out the misstep.

If we are the ones dishing out the "this is where you got it wrong" input, our job is to find the most effective way to deliver the message. It begins with assessing whether our listener is even ready for rerouting. We might not make that sing-song Waze sound, but it is our task to communicate according to the others' need. We can ask ourselves: *What are the words this child can hear? How might my spouse need me to respond right now?* Sometimes, we will choose not to comment at all. The timing, tone, and content of our message will directly influence the receptivity of our listener. When we feel attacked, we shut down. When we feel loved and understood, we can be open to feedback.

And, if we are the ones requiring some life recalculating, our task is to welcome the notifications. We'd lodge a list of complaints if our GPS let us drive the wrong way. We ought to likewise expect those we trust to give us the pointers we need to stay on course. I'm hoping Waze does find a way to offer a latte en route. Until then, it's on us to find compassionate ways of recalculating.

## YOUR TURN: GUIDE QUESTIONS

- How do you communicate nonverbally? What is your body language when you are listening to someone? Can you experiment with a more open posture? Better eye contact? How can you convey that you are really listening to your loved ones?
- Are there times or situations where you find yourself gossiping or using speech in a negative way? How can you set aside time each day to be careful about how you speak? What can you do to strengthen your resolve to be a careful talker at these more vulnerable times?
- Who do you see on a daily basis? Who are the "acquaintances" in your life? Is there a way you can take responsibility for brightening their world? Perhaps you smile at your doorman or ask how the cashier is doing. What shifts when you see each person in front of you as an opportunity?
- Where do you long for more connection and a deeper relationship? Instead of running from this yearning, can you use it to direct your life? How can you bring more meaningful connection into your days?

# CHAPTER 9

# Love

> "A person comes to love the one to whom he gives…the
> only reason the other person seems a stranger to him is
> because he has not yet given to him."
>
> (Rabbi Eliyahu Eliezer Dessler, *Kuntrus Hachessed*)

*"Whoever is fearful and fainthearted should go and return
to his home."*

*(Devarim 20:8)*

There he was, dangling right before me. At first, I hardly saw him, but then there was no missing his presence—suspended directly at eye level. In all his creepy-crawly splendor, he was an unwelcome visitor: a spider.

I'm no spider lover. That said, if there is no one else in the room, I will manage to "take care of business."

I realized that I was close to a doorway and, beyond wishing his presence gone, I also noticed there might be a slightly less fatal way to achieve this end. It would require some fancy door opening and gentle spider-scooping action on my part. So, I ran to get the necessary paraphernalia and propped open the door. Upon my return, he had inched ever so slightly higher along the thread of his web but was not lost from my gaze. Operation Arachnid Rescue was underway. With one swift scoop, a gentle grasp, and the willingness to let go of the spider, I sent him into his natural habitat.

Freeing the creatures around us to return to where they belong requires a gentle touch. It's one thing to let go of a spider; it's another to let go in relationships. It can be difficult to allow our children and spouses the space they need. We tend to hold on tighter when we get scared. When we wish someone would change or we sense them pulling away, we feel anxious and out of control. We try to fix them in an attempt to alleviate our own discomfort. Jumping into action, we nag, push, and even force ourselves and our opinions on others.

If you're nodding your head, you know this strategy rarely works. In fact, it backfires, pushing people away and driving a wedge between loved ones. There may be a time to act or give advice, but never from a place of fear and anxiety.

When we are calm and grounded, we can connect. We can think through how to love and support according to *the other*'s needs. Sometimes, that means stepping back, giving them space, or even letting go. When fear runs the show, we are single-minded, thinking only, *How do I get this out now?!* We tend to crush the creature in the lifting, leaving little to salvage other than a crumpled mess where once there was life. If this is true of spiders, it is equally true in relationships.

I released that spider and watched him crawl along the path. Who knows what the breeze, a pedestrian, or the rest of the day brought him. I had to let go. I helped him return to his home. In my fear, I could have squashed him, squeezed so tight as to have been fatal. But instead, a gentle transfer led to another moment of life—for us both. A life and even a day without moments of fear might be impossible, but we *can* avoid crushing the spirits of those we love.

When we are overcome with the desire to micromanage other people's lives, we can choose to be quiet or ask supportive questions, sending the message, "I believe in your ability to figure this out." If we feel someone growing distant, we can respect the space they need, or communicate from a place of calm and connection. Sometimes the truest love *is* setting someone free, giving both parties permission to move independently.

The game changer is really what we do when we find ourselves eye to eye with the spider moments of life: Do we panic into action and smother, or do we gently scoop up ourselves, our lives, and our loved ones?

*"Two are better than one because they have a good reward for their labor. For if they fall, the one will lift up his fellow."*
*(Koheles 4:9–10)*

I love a good first-base coach. Let me tell you why. In baseball, when a batter reaches first base, waiting for him is a coach, whose job it is to greet him on arrival and provide guidance (to run to second or stay at first).

I watch for the moment the two make contact. The first-base coach for the Toronto Blue Jays, Tim Leiper, has the sweetest smile. He looks like the kind of guy you'd like to invite over for dinner. I revel in his greeting of each runner. There is kindness, a comradery.

I study their faces as they speak. I guess they're talking about the game, what to look out for, the next move. Perhaps they're chatting about post-game dinner plans or clubhouse banter.

What the team enacts on the field is the not-so-simple art of humanity: connecting and strategizing on the field of life. However, the coach's job is not to keep the player on base. In fact, he quickly gets busy sending him on his way.

A friend recently told me about a custom in some African cultures called a "push." When a guest leaves, the host will walk the guest on her way, sometimes all the way home, and this is described as a push. At times, once the guest has arrived home, she will in turn start walking her host back along the road, thus returning the push.

Roads can get bumpy and transitions are tough. Sometimes our tired souls need a gentle boost. In the Torah, we learn this from Avraham, who not only welcomed guests into his tent, but also escorted them out. With a few footsteps, he aided their transition to the journey ahead, letting them know that even in leaving, they were not alone. We also learn this from those magical first-base coaches.

We all need a smiling face greeting us when we make it to our destination. We all need a "push" of encouragement to continue striving. And yes, we all need some advice and comradery. Imagine having a personal first-base coach there with you throughout your day. He'd be there in your kitchen giving you a thumbs-up as you leave the house—lunches made, and kids fed, bathed, and dressed. He'd give you a gentle, "You got this!" in the mid-afternoon when your to-do list or work project starts to feel overwhelming. And just when the voice of "I'm not sure I can keep going" creeps in, he would walk a few steps with you until you got your stride back.

If we all need a first-base coach, we can also be that person in someone else's life. We can be the one who recognizes efforts and believes that even if it's been a rough go or a season-long slump, great things are on the horizon. Our life is full of players looking to make their way from one base to another. More often than not, they are fighting private battles and struggling to keep going. We may not see it at first, but if we become skilled coaches, we'll recognize the needs of others around us. We will come to know a face that longs for encouragement and a heart that needs to be heard. None of us can make the journey without help, no one can overcome obstacles alone. We can be the game-changing force in another's life.

The first-base coach doesn't leave his post. It's not about his personal glory. His honor is in the push itself. That can be ours as well. If you look carefully, you'll find your day filled with coaching moments.

I'll see you out there on the field.

There is a charm to secondhand bookstores largely lost in this age of box stores and online shopping. Still, Amazon has a way of preserving the mystique of previously loved books: the used-book option. There are risks when you go that way—yes, the price might be shockingly lower, but the item may be in equally poor condition. Sometimes, I live on the edge. I order the used copy and wait for my brown Amazon-labeled box to arrive.

The neat thing about a used book is that it holds two stories. The one upon its pages, inscribed by the author, and the other left behind by its previous reader. I once found a cookbook with a note to a bride on her wedding day. Another time, I leafed through a philosophy text with questions written in the margins. Did the reader ever find what they were looking for?

We second-round readers can't know the answers. So maybe there is a third story: the one we fill in; the places we insert our own assumptions about those who have owned before us, our fellow phantom readers. I had this pleasure as I recently thumbed through a new-to-me purchase. While *Dialectical Behavior Therapy in Clinical Practice* may not be everyone's idea of a page turner, I was pretty psyched (no pun intended). These hardcover editions can set you back quite a bit, so the "good condition" promise convinced me to buy a used copy.

Flipping between chapters, a paper fell into my lap. I felt like I'd stumbled upon buried treasure. I picked it up. A Borders Books and Music store receipt. Dated July 31, 2011. In Mission Viejo, California. My mind raced. Where exactly is Mission Viejo? And the other item on the bill? A book titled, *Most Notorious Crimes*. Who in the world was the purchaser? A crime-loving psychologist? A forensic detective? A student? What was happening in their life at that time and day that made those two books in a West Coast store the needed items of the moment?

The bill became magical, creating a bridge between me and an anonymous Californian book buyer. I will never know their name, but I felt connected. Why? Because I imagined. I became curious. I started to wonder what their universe was about. Which meant I had a brief reprieve from my own.

If secondhand bookstores are an endangered species, their lessons are worth grabbing now. Like those books, each of us carry multiple stories. We are all fighting a private battle, managing unexpected chapters, and making our way sentence by sentence.

Like that Borders' bill drifting into my lap, each person we encounter is an invitation to connect. When we see the layers of stories around us, we likewise discover untapped needs. Standing face-to-face with someone, we can put ourselves in their shoes and imagine what they might need.

See the stress in a friend's eyes? Ask her how she is doing. Notice the sniffle of a stranger? Pass a tissue. Each time we get curious about someone else's story, we open the door to connection. Every time we respond by giving, we walk through that opening, becoming a little more invested in one another and a drop more connected.

We are in the business of building love through giving. Maybe that Borders' receipt came to remind me, and us, that we need not remain strangers. I will never meet that unsuspecting Borders shopper; I can't say thank you or give a smile. Our connection is tenuous at best. But we will all come upon many people who need us to imagine their world, call us to notice their need, and invite us to give. For now, I'm going to keep choosing the "used" option on Amazon and dreaming of all those stories around me.

*"A time to weep and a time to laugh."*

*(Koheles 3:4)*

Every year, I'm pretty sure it will be the last. Funny Hat Day, that is.

My first year as a mom of a preschooler, my daughter came home with a notice salvaged from the bottom of the school bag. In honor of Rosh Chodesh Adar, the beginning of the Hebrew month of Adar, children were to come to school with "funny hats."

Rosh Chodesh Adar is a time in the calendar year when we increase our joy. It's also two weeks before Purim, and thus a day when we start to get our "happy" on. So, we rummaged through our costume bin and sent her off with appropriate head paraphernalia.

By the next year, I was ready. When that notice came home, I knew what to expect. We laid out the hat choices the night before. *We were prepared.* Except we weren't, because the next morning came with a fever and a new reality. What's a mother to do? You guessed it—stage Funny Hat Day at home!

Of course, it's no fun if you're wearing goofy headwear alone. So obviously, the rest of us had to follow suit. Picture the scene: a family sitting down to supper (only one child present), tiaras and cowboy hats on each head. In this, our annual tradition was born. Given that my favorite part of kindergarten was the dress-up corner, I have no complaints.

Each time Adar approaches and I casually mention that, "it's almost Funny Hat Day time," I expect the reaction to be, "It's too babyish." Fair. So, every time we once again don our ridiculous getups, I try to bottle the hilarity, knowing that soon it will be "what we used to do."

Children have a way of giving us permission to dust off our silly side. You only need to look at an adult making ridiculous faces at a baby to see this power. But they grow up. And that's their job. Which means dress up at dinner is time-limited.

Somewhere mid-meal I mention that this will probably be our last Funny Hat Day. But so far, I've been wrong. I don't know if I'm jinxing things by sharing this. We've upped our game this year—we're sending an Evite to the event (which means we're inviting the three people we live with). I suppose that's the art of growing with the times—making room for new within the old. I'm OK with that. I might even be OK with a new tradition.

It's so easy to lapse into routines and lose the novelty—in life and in love. It would be simple enough to say, "We've been doing it this way, it's always worked, why do we have to change?" Or we might give up the ritual completely, dismissing the experience as something that "we used to do." The magic's gone and therefore so are we.

When it comes to retiring Funny Hat Day, the consequences would be minor. We'd pack away the costumes along with the memories. Yet, we take this approach in more fundamental areas—parenting, marriage, and our spirituality. We find a way to do something, a habit, and we relax into a groove. And then it starts to lose its zing. We get bored.

Routine is the enemy of relationship. We are wired to love newness. That's why last year's fashions no longer excite; it's the reason we are drawn to beginnings and fresh starts. We grow apathetic when we feel like there's nothing new to discover or experience. If routine can be fatal, then novelty is its antidote, the key to keeping any relationship alive. This is as true when it comes to marriage as it is in our relationships with our friends, our work, and our Creator.

Don't be mistaken; we don't disregard the old or run from the familiar in our pursuit of newness. In fact, we treasure hard-won trust and the deep sense of security that comes from long-term relationships. Yet within those bonds, we need constant opportunities for renewal, ways to "up our game" and a shared commitment to growing with the times. This can sound like serious business. Yet anyone peering in at the scene of our annual Funny Hat Day would argue otherwise. Making room for new within the old can be a lot of fun. It can be goofy or exciting. It can make a been-there-done-that relationship alive all over again. And that, I believe, is a tradition worth keeping.

Interesting, how our minds will automatically fill in missing information.

Driving on the highway, I passed a skating rink with a sign that read, "Town rena." Without skipping a beat, my brain filled in the missing "A." I didn't even puzzle for a moment to wonder what on earth a "rena" could be. In a neuronal nanosecond, I had read and accommodated for the missing information. I could do this because I have a mental catalog that includes skating rinks and signage. With this background knowledge and experience, even a missing vowel didn't change much about the sign.

We read incomplete signs every day—our brains are wired to encounter an incomplete world. Built right into our cognitive processing is the ability to survey an imperfect word—and world—and fill in what is missing.

Who knows how long that letter 'A' has been missing from the skating rink? Perhaps some kids pulled it off as part of a prank or the simple wear and tear of weather left it at the bottom of a pile of junk.

More important than the lettering on random buildings, life will present us with scenarios that appear short of essential pieces. Our days are punctuated by what's missing: the dryer eating half our socks, not enough time to get everything done, or finding the coffee pot empty just when you really needed a java fix. Sometimes our deficiencies scream even louder: not enough love, health, patience, or money to pay that looming bill. How we approach those missing pieces will determine the course of our lives.

As surely as letters fall from signs, this world is made of broken hearts and fractured dreams. It is the essence of the human soul to look at the brokenness around us and long to fix it. If our brains are wired to fill in the missing data, our souls are formed to fill the gaping holes of imperfection. Healing this world doesn't have to take the form of "big banner efforts," such as starting an organization, raising money, or feeding the poor. Sometimes, it's simply noticing when someone needs a hug, saying a kind hello, or holding the door open. These may seem like small acts. They are. Small doesn't mean insignificant. If a single missing letter can change an entire word, one kind gesture can fill a soul-size hole.

The challenge is to read the signs of life slowly enough to notice what's missing. It takes skill to give someone exactly what they lack; it takes a keen eye to see who needs you. Our deficiencies are different, our needs are unique. What we do have in common is a soul wired to fill in the blanks. The good news? Every day is filled with opportunities to practice: needy people, hungry bellies, and missing vowels to be filled. Last time I drove by that rink, the 'A' was still missing. I suppose it's a fitting reminder to keeping looking for those holes.

She drove into the pharmacy parking lot the wrong way, through the exit. There I was at the entrance, second car in line, waiting for a spot to free up, and *she* zipped in the other end and claimed the first free spot. Can you imagine?

I was annoyed, brimming with the sort of self-righteous indignation reserved for parking lots. So, when the driver ahead of me (who had been cheated of his rightful spot) rolled down his window and began gesticulating, I didn't mind. I mean, someone *needed* to let her know that it was not OK to swoop in the exit and claim a spot. I watched as she walked by my car. We made eye contact.

Eventually, I found a spot and made my way into the pharmacy. Somewhere between the prescription drop-off and the shampoo aisle we once again crossed paths. Again, we momentarily locked eyes. I don't know if it was my imagination, but she seemed to offer a sheepish smile.

With fifteen minutes to spare until my prescription would be ready, I ran across the street to accomplish one more errand. Stepping out of the store, there she was—again! And again, we exchanged a look. Something about her seemed familiar. *Does she know me?* I wondered. Is she embarrassed, realizing I witnessed her parking lot transgression? Was that look a glance of guilt or acknowledgement?

Somewhere mid-street it struck me: she may well have known what she did. There may have been little to defend in her act. But who am I kidding? I also go the wrong way sometimes—if not in the pharmacy lot, most certainly as I steer through life. Maybe the look she gave me was not denying her misstep, but an appeal to let it slide this time. It was as if her eyes were begging, "Go easy on me, please." I'm not talking about judging her favorably here—doing mental gymnastics to come up with a rationale for her act: emergencies at home, unseen adversity, or ignorance that she entered through the exit. I am going on the premise that she was in a rush, wanted that spot, and took it. Out of turn. On purpose. But each time we locked eyes, she became a little less of a "parking spot thief" and a little more human. In exchange, maybe I became a drop more human too.

We build ourselves protective forts of judgment. If you don't live up to my expectations, I hold you responsible for letting me down. What if I would respond with compassion when you get it wrong instead of exacting judgment? What if I smiled back at guilty eyes, letting them know, "Honey, I've been there, too." Maybe next time my own imperfection surfaces, someone will likewise turn away, or at least exchange an understanding smile in the parking lot of life.

I didn't see her again. I don't know if she felt judged or forgiven.

Still, I felt changed. Parking lot drama will be among life's more minor missteps. But every time we overlook a small transgression, each time we soften in the face of someone else's failure, we get to be a little bit more like G-d. It doesn't mean anything goes. There are rights and wrongs, check and balances. But there are also opportunities to say, "I get it." I'm human. I make mistakes. I also need a forgiving smile. So, next time we catch each other on a difficult day, I hope we will all be able to lock eyes in our common imperfection. As for the Parking Lot Lady, I'm hoping we cross paths soon. It'll be one more chance to practice my "I get it" smile.

*"Receive everyone with a cheerful countenance."*

**(Pirkei Avos 1:15)**

There are some family traditions with which you just don't mess. Rituals we follow because that's just how it's done.

One of our tried-and-true traditions is the "Welcome Home" sign. We are strict when it comes to the guidelines: Any time a family member has traveled, been away for a stretch of time, or returned from a noteworthy voyage, a sign is required to greet their return.

As a child, I recall the emergence of poster board and magic markers heralding the end of winter. Bubby and Zaidie would be coming home from Miami, and we were entrusted with the job of making the sign. As time marched on, the signs evolved. Computer graphics, balloons, and even an irreverent "This Is a Welcome Home Sign," note has graced our doorway.

You'd think we would come to expect it, and I suppose we do. But even though this is what we do in our family, I remain pleasantly surprised to find such signage greeting me.

This is not a campaign to promote Welcome Home signs. I would guess that there are heads nodding with equally treasured, must-keep family traditions. It's not a matter of magic markers or shiny stickers, but it is about a kind of magic.

The world out there can be tough. We can spend all day trying to make it, hustle, and accomplish. None of this is bad. We need grit and gumption for life, but we also need a soft place to land. We tell kids to use their "indoor voices" because we also need an outdoor voice. It is important to have a version of ourselves that can keep up with a noisy world. That's part of our life's work—to learn how to make it "out there." To have some street smarts. To manage the twists and turns and bumps on the road.

But then, we need a home. A door that will open and say: *You are here. You are safe. Come in. I'm happy you are back. I missed you.* Sometimes it's a physical door. Sometimes there are people to make those signs. And, sometimes we need to be the sign makers ourselves.

How often do we greet the people who walk in the door of our homes, workplaces, and lives? Do we run to our kids, friends, and spouses to say, "You belong here! I am happy to see you?" Or are we too busy on the phone or in our head to even make eye contact? Making Welcome Home signs is an experience of who we can be: the gatekeepers of connection. When we say hello, locking eyes with a smile, we are saying, "I see you, I care. You can use your indoor self with me."

The world will call to us, and we will need to step up and out into the bustle of life. As we make our way out there, we can make others feel at home. The signs we send to the world through our words and our gestures can create islands of connection and safety. We don't need to be standing at a doorway to make someone feel at home. We are surrounded by opportunities to care for others; if you start looking you will find them everywhere.

Hold the door for a stranger. Strike up a conversation with the checkout lady. Take the time to ask a friend how she's really doing. Developing this awareness is a habit we can build as an everyday practice. We can become welcome sign detectives, looking for ways to make others feel safe and loved. That's where the magic happens. So, next time your kid walks through the door or you pass a stranger on the street, you may just find yourself in the business of proverbial sign making. I'll meet you out there with the magic markers.

─────────── YOUR TURN: GUIDE QUESTIONS ───────────

- Is there a relationship where you have fallen into a routine? Do you wish you felt more of that energy and newness you once had? How can you reinvigorate your connection? Set aside time to be together. Find a new way to spend time with your spouse. Take your kids on a local adventure.

- Is there someone in your life who needs more encouragement? Try sharing encouraging words with that person once a day—it can be in person, a note, or a message. How does your relationship change? How does their sense of confidence develop?

- Next time you are in a public space or social gathering, look around you. Who could use a bit of "TLC," some love and support? How can you make someone near you feel cared for? Offering a kind word, a drink of water, or a smile can be the boost someone needs.

- What resources has G-d given you? Is it energy, money, creativity, a love of cooking? How can you transform this into giving? Who can you share with?

# Conclusion

Each story in this book follows a structure; you may have found it. Here it is:

1. I share a story or observation of the world.
2. I have an initial reaction based on what I expect to find, or how I think things should go.
3. I ask: What is the lesson here? What is another way to look at this? Where is the wisdom in this moment? What is my choice?
4. I choose to look for a way up—to find meaning, growth, and G-d in my experience.
5. My experience is transformed—I feel more joy and can make more deliberate choices about how I think, speak, and act.

Now it's your turn. Time to make "choosing up" your daily practice. Time to write *your* book. Here's the first page:

1. What is something you experienced this past week that was interesting? Challenging? Imperfect?
2. What was your initial reaction or judgment?
3. What is a different way to look at this?
4. How are you going to choose up? Where can you find meaning, growth, and G-d?
5. How will this change how you think, speak, and act?

Go for it!

# About the Author

Ilana Kendal is a psychotherapist, occupational therapist, teacher, and author. As an international lecturer and gifted storyteller, Ilana mines Jewish wisdom for its relevance to our personal paths and struggles. Her writing can be found on aish.com, chabad.org, kveller.com, and in her weekly email, where she reveals profound messages through everyday experiences. In her psychotherapy and occupational therapy practice, she works with individuals through life transitions, mood disorders, and eating disorders. Ilana is passionate about creating environments of empowerment and fostering personal growth. She lives in Toronto with her family. For more about Ilana's work, visit www.ilanakendal.com.

*In honor of*
*the Rabbis and Rebbetzins, the teachers and students,*
*the congregants and guests of*

# The Village Shul

*who enrich our lives and create space for beautiful*
*books such as this one.*
*With great admiration,*

Ronnie, Debra, Shira, and Yarden Aronson

---

*In honor of*

# Yisroel ben Avraham, z"l,
# our Zaida and patriarch

*who survived the loss of his parents at a young age,*
*who as the oldest child supported his siblings, who*
*survived the Holocaust but lost much of his family, and*
*who moved forward to start a new life and legacy—in*
*his business and in his family—for future generations.*
*A man who "always looked up" and moved forward.*

*May his memory be a blessing to all who came*
*before him, and to all who are standing*
*on his shoulders today.*

Barry and Donna Bank

*In memory of*

# Bubbie and Zaidy
# Jean and Abe Diamond

*of blessed memory*

*In our tradition, memory is valued and sanctified because its ultimate purpose is to propel us to some sort of action or deed. In remembering how these two loving and giving people always chose a life of goodness, love, and Jewish values after living through unimaginable darkness, we are inspired by them to choose how to live our lives. Their legacy is to always choose up.*

*May our growing family be guided by their memories, inspired by their wisdom, optimism, strength, and humility, so all of our steps forward will bring us the blessings of Hashem.*

Mom, Dad, Sarah, Omri, Zoe, Isla, Marc, Shevi, and Darya
Uncle Elliott, Aunt Rochelle, Avi, Sonia, Miri, Kayla, Yaakov, Zalman, Rikki, Alexander, Eliana, Amiel, Ahuva, Menashe Hillel, Yitzi, and Efraim

---

*In memory of*

# Faigy Hoch

*A true eishes chayil*

*A woman who gave of her true heart and soul to her family and community, and who inspired with her modesty, humility, warmth, and authenticity. She was a light to all she touched.*

Sandy Herlick and Jack Frieberg

*In memory of our grandfathers*

# Philip (Pinchas) Rosenblatt and Josef (Yosef Shlomo) Motzen

*Two men who exemplified the values of this book—men, who in their own unique way, struggled against adversity and never stopped fighting for more: more life, more spirituality, and more love.*

*The lives of these two great people serve as an eternal inspiration to all who knew them and may the teachings of this book do the same.*

Chaim, A.D., Yitz, Bella, Yisrael, and Shmuli Motzen

---

*Dedicated to the memory of*

# Beverly Diana Tepperman (Bayla Dina bas Moshe)

*who lived each day of her life with the greatest amount of joy, selflessness, and love. She showed others, especially her family, what it truly means to be a fighter and to embrace challenges with a smile and laugh. Her unique spirit and energy are missed everyday by all who knew her.*

Arthur and Ellie Stern and family

In honor of my beloved father

# Phillip Young

## Pesach ben Yosef, a"h

*May his memory be for a blessing.*

*Ilana, I am so proud of you on the publication
of your first book.*

Bernita Young

---

*In memory of my dad*

# Shlomo ben Reuven, zt"l

Susan Zehavi

# With gratitude to all the supporters who made this book possible

Karen Birbrager
Michael and Tara Bloom
Brenda Borenstein
Faye Davis
Leonard and Judy Direnfeld
Shoshana Fishberg
Emanuel Flatt and Jillian Rodak
Peter and Eva Friedmann
Philip and Sara Goldband
Marcel Jakubovic and Erin Gano
Susan Jarnicki
Gary and Lynne Jonsohn
Allan Kaplan and Cheryl Reicin
Asher and Jordana Lichtman
Sanford and Marsha Meyers
Bernie and Michal Moskoff
Linda Nardea
Sharon Neiss Arbess
Zale and Rochel Newman
Lou, a"h, and Mary Orzech
Moshe and Claire Oziel
Tessa Rubenstein
Sappho by Kim Smiley Inc.
Brian and Robbie Schwartz
Rachel Sheps
Shmuel and Elana Soroka
Adam Starkman and Michelle Garshon
The Strasser Family
Marliz Tel
Nada Thompson
Jory and Joan Vernon
Robert and Shauna Walker
The Weitz Family Foundation